First World War
and Army of Occupation
War Diary
France, Belgium and Germany

51 DIVISION
Divisional Troops
Divisional Ammunition Column
17 April 1915 - 31 March 1919

WO95/2854/8

The Naval & Military Press Ltd
www.nmarchive.com
Published in association with The National Archives

Published by

The Naval & Military Press Ltd

Unit 10 Ridgewood Industrial Park,
Uckfield, East Sussex,
TN22 5QE England
Tel: +44 (0) 1825 749494

www.naval-military-press.com

www.nmarchive.com

This diary has been reprinted in facsimile from the original. Any imperfections are inevitably reproduced and the quality may fall short of modern type and cartographic standards.

© Crown Copyright
Images reproduced by permission of The National Archives, London, England, 2015.

Contents

Document type	Place/Title	Date From	Date To
War Diary	Carvin	01/06/1915	26/06/1915
War Diary	Estairs	27/06/1915	27/06/1915
Heading	WO95/2854/8 (51 Div) Dnnl Ammunition Train 1915 April-1919 March		
Heading	51st Division 51st Divl. Ammn Column Apr 1915-Mar 1919		
Heading	51st Division. 51st Divl. Ammn. Col. Vol 1		
War Diary	Bedford	17/04/1915	17/04/1915
War Diary	Blackheath	20/04/1915	03/05/1915
War Diary	Woolwich	04/05/1915	04/05/1915
War Diary	Southampton	05/05/1915	05/05/1915
War Diary	Havre	06/05/1915	07/05/1915
War Diary	Berguette Hamit Billet	08/05/1915	09/05/1915
War Diary	Robecq	10/05/1915	14/05/1915
War Diary	Padrelles	14/05/1915	15/05/1915
War Diary	La Borgue Paradis	18/05/1915	26/05/1915
War Diary	Cornet Malo	27/05/1915	30/05/1915
War Diary	Carvin	31/05/1915	31/05/1915
War Diary	Estairs	01/07/1915	29/07/1915
War Diary	Bussy Les Daours	30/07/1915	31/07/1915
Heading	51st List. Ammn Coln Vol 11 Aug Sep 1 Oct 15		
War Diary	Bussy Les Daours	01/08/1915	07/08/1915
War Diary	Bavelin Court	08/08/1915	21/10/1915
Heading	51st Divnl Ammn Col Nov 1915 Vol III		
War Diary	Bavelin Court	01/11/1915	30/11/1915
Heading	51st Divnl Ammn Col Dec Vol IV		
War Diary	Bavelin Court	01/12/1915	29/12/1915
Heading	51 High Div Ammn Col Jan 1916 Vol V		
War Diary	Bavel In Court	01/01/1916	08/01/1916
War Diary	Arboe Uves	09/01/1916	31/01/1916
War Diary	Bavel In Court	01/01/1916	08/01/1916
War Diary	Arboe Uves	09/01/1916	31/01/1916
War Diary	Bavel In Court	01/01/1916	08/01/1916
War Diary	Argoeuves	09/01/1916	07/02/1916
War Diary	Sailly-Le-Sec	08/02/1916	27/02/1916
War Diary	Villers Bocage	29/02/1916	03/03/1916
War Diary	Hem	06/03/1916	08/03/1916
War Diary	Rebreuves	09/03/1916	10/03/1916
War Diary	Berlancourt Bois D'Habarcq	11/03/1916	14/03/1916
War Diary	Tilloy	15/03/1916	15/03/1916
War Diary	Berles	16/03/1916	31/03/1916
War Diary	Monchel Berles	01/04/1916	31/05/1916
Miscellaneous	With War Diary For May, 1916	06/05/1916	06/05/1916
War Diary	Monchel Berles	01/06/1916	11/06/1916
War Diary	Agnieres	12/06/1916	30/06/1916
Heading	War Diary Of 51st Divl Ammunition Column From 1st July 1916 To 31st July 1916 (Volume XI)		
War Diary	Agnieres	01/07/1916	31/07/1916
Heading	51st Divisional Artillery 51st Divisional Ammunition Column R.F.A. August 1916		

War Diary	Meaulte	01/08/1916	20/08/1916
War Diary	Pont-De-Nieppe	21/08/1916	31/08/1916
Heading	War Diary Of 51st (Highland) Divisional Ammunition Column R.F.A. September 1916 Vol 13		
War Diary	Steenwerck	09/01/1916	26/01/1916
War Diary	Anvin	27/09/1916	30/09/1916
Heading	War Diary Of 51st (Highland) Divisional Provisional Column RFA For October 1916 Vol 14		
War Diary	Puchevillers	01/10/1916	07/10/1916
War Diary	Louvencourt	08/10/1916	24/10/1916
War Diary	Thievres	25/10/1916	31/10/1916
Heading	War Diary Of 51st (Highland) Divisional Ammunition Column R.F.A. For November 1916 Vol 15		
War Diary	Thievres	01/11/1916	25/11/1916
War Diary	Field	25/11/1916	30/11/1916
Heading	War Diary Of 51st (Highland) Divisional Ammunition Column R.F.A. For December, 1916 Vol 16		
War Diary	Brickfields Area (W.16. B. Combd Sht)	01/12/1916	19/12/1916
War Diary	Brickfields Area	20/12/1916	31/12/1916
Heading	War Diary Of 51st (Highland) Division Ammunition Column R.F.A. For January 1917 Vol 17		
War Diary	Field	01/01/1917	31/01/1917
Heading	War Diary Of 51st (Highland) Divisional Ammunition Column R.F.A. For February, 1917 Vol 18		
War Diary	Novelles S. Mer	01/02/1917	28/02/1917
Heading	War Diary Of 51st (Highland) Divisional Ammunition Column R.F.A. For March 1917 Vol 19		
War Diary	Field	01/03/1917	31/03/1917
Heading	War Diary Of 51st (Highland) Divisional Ammunition Column R.F.A. For April 1917 Vol 20		
War Diary	Field	01/04/1917	30/04/1917
Heading	War Diary Of 51st (Highland) Divisional Ammunition Column R.F.A. For May 1917 Vol 21		
War Diary	Field	01/05/1917	31/05/1917
Heading	War Diary Of 51st (Highland) Divisional Ammunition Column For June 1917 Vol 22		
War Diary	Field	01/06/1917	30/06/1917
Heading	War Diary Of 51st (Highland) Divisional Ammunition Column, R.F.A. For July, 1917 Vol 23		
War Diary	Field	01/07/1917	31/07/1917
Heading	War Diary Of 51st (Highland) Divisional Amm Col R.F.A. For August 1917 Vol 24		
War Diary	Field	01/08/1917	31/08/1917
Heading	War Diary Of 51st (Highland) Divisional Ammunition Column For September 1917 Vol 25		
War Diary	Field	01/09/1917	30/09/1917
Heading	War Diary Of 51st (Highland) Divisional Ammunition Column. R.F.A. For October, 1917 Vol 26		
War Diary	Field	01/10/1917	31/10/1917
Heading	War Diary Of 51st (Highland) Divisional Ammunition Column, R.F.A. For November, 1917 Vol 27		
War Diary	Field	01/11/1917	30/11/1917
Heading	War Diary Of 51st D.A.C For December 1917 Vol 28		
War Diary	Field	01/12/1917	31/12/1917
Heading	War Diary Of 51st D.A.C. For January, 1918 Vol 29		
War Diary	Field	01/01/1918	30/01/1918

Heading	War Diary Of 51st D.A.C. For February, 1918 Vol 30		
War Diary	Field	01/02/1918	28/02/1918
Heading	War Diary Of 51st D.A.C. For March 1918 Vol 31		
War Diary	Field	01/03/1918	31/03/1918
Heading	51st Divisional Artillery 51st Divisional Ammunition Column R.F.A. April 1918		
Heading	War Diary Of 51st D.A.C. For April, 1918 Vol 32		
War Diary	Field	01/04/1918	30/04/1918
Heading	War Diary Of 51st D.A.C. For May, 1918 Vol 33		
War Diary	Field	01/05/1918	31/05/1918
Heading	War Diary Of 51st D.A.C. For June 1918 Vol 34		
War Diary	Field	01/06/1918	30/06/1918
Heading	Divisional Artillery 51st (Highland) Division 51st Divisional Ammunition Column July, 1918		
War Diary	Field	01/07/1918	31/07/1918
Heading	War Diary Of 51st D.A.C. For August 1918 Vol 36		
War Diary	Field	01/08/1918	31/08/1918
Heading	War Diary Of 51st D.A.C. For September, 1918 Vol 37		
War Diary	Field	01/09/1918	30/09/1918
Heading	War Diary October 1918 51st (Highland) Div Amm. Col R.F.A. Vol 38		
War Diary	Field	01/10/1918	31/10/1918
Heading	War Diary Of 51st D.A.C. For November, 1918 Vol 39		
War Diary	Fields	01/11/1918	30/11/1918
Miscellaneous	War Diary Of 51st D.A.C. For December 1918		
War Diary	Field	01/12/1918	31/12/1918
Heading	War Diary Of 51st D.A.C. For January, 1919 Vol 41		
War Diary	Fields	01/01/1919	31/01/1919
Heading	War Diary Of 51st D.A.C. For February 1919 Vol 43		
War Diary	Field	01/02/1919	28/02/1919
Heading	War Diary 51st D.A.C March 1919 Vol 43		
War Diary	Field	01/03/1919	31/03/1919

Army Form C. 2118.

WAR DIARY
INTELLIGENCE SUMMARY.
(Erase heading not required.)

51st (High'd) Divisional Amm Col.

Place	Date	Hour	Summary of Events and Information	Remarks and references to Appendices
	1915			
CARVIN	1 to 25		Still at Billet - learning daily ammunition to B'dge Amm Cols, daily routine, Physical Drill, Exercising horses, marching horses, marching rifle Drill, signalling, map reading, Lectures, Route marches, Bathing Parades	2.v.p.
	26	2.45pm	Received orders to move - arrived ESTAIRS 6 p.m.	2.v.p.
ESTAIRS	27 to 30		Still at Billet, General Routine, daily supply of ammunition to B'dge Amm Cols, Drill as before.	2.v.p.

WO 95 2854/8

(51 DIV) DIVNL. AMMUNITION TRAIN

1915 APRIL - 1919 MARCH

51ST DIVISION

51ST DIVL, AMMN COLUMN
APR 1915 - MAR 1919

51ST DIVISION

12/6357

51ˢᵗ Division

51st Divl: Auun " Pla

Vol I.
4-4-31-7-15

Army Form C. 2118.

WAR DIARY
INTELLIGENCE SUMMARY.

(Erase heading not required.)

51st (Highland) Division Ammunition Col.

Instructions regarding War Diaries and Intelligence Summaries are contained in F.S. Regs, Part II. and the Staff Manual respectively. Title pages will be prepared in manuscript.

Place	Date	Hour	Summary of Events and Information	Remarks and references to Appendices
Bedford	April 1915 17	11.30 am	Instructions received to form Highland Divisional Ammunition Column. Lieut. Col. Cm Lloyd Robertson, 4" Highland (India) Bde. R.F.A. appointed O.C. and Capt. L.M. Annand of Bute Battery 4" Highland (India) Bde. R.F.A. appointed Adjutant. One officer & 90 N.C. Os & men of 1st & 2nd Lincs Bde Battery received as first instalment of personnel.	R.W.D.
	19		Left Bedford 7 a.m. arrives BLACKHEATH at 11 a.m. when mobilization fitting out took place at No 2 Reserve Horse Transport Depôt	R.W.D.
BLACKHEATH	20		mobilization tables received. Individuals made out nominatus. Harness equipment stores drawn from Woolwich - all parts of harness rtc'd - sorted out & returned as weights recdts & sections. Wagons received from Transport Depôt & numbers N.O. arrives	R.W.D.
	27		Clothing equipment receiving received.	R.W.D.
	28		Continuation of sorting out of harness & stores equipment - first batch of mules returned over them. Fitting of harness to officers arrives	R.W.D.
	29		Ammunition received from Arsenal calculated to the waterline. M.O. arrives & 2 other Riding horses transport horses received calculates & sections. Sorting out, fitting of harness	R.W.D.
	30		Further quinto arrives - fitting of harness to teams recommences equipment stores returning same	R.W.D.

Army Form C. 2118.

WAR DIARY
INTELLIGENCE SUMMARY.
(Erase heading not required.)

51st (Highld) Division at Arm. Col.

Instructions regarding War Diaries and Intelligence Summaries are contained in F. S. Regs., Part II and the Staff Manual respectively. Title pages will be prepared in manuscript.

Place	Date	Hour	Summary of Events and Information	Remarks and references to Appendices
	Aug 1915			
BLACKHEATH	1 to 3		Continuation of mobilization - Remainder of above regiment returned from Woolwich with stores & lorries - inadequate equipment footware - Remainder of officers arrived to complete full Establishment. Remainder of units arrived - Establishment complete.	2wa
WOOLWICH	4	10am 3.30	Strength Parade on 2nd & 3rd when whole Column entrained for Southampton. Received orders to proceed overseas. Baggage and first section left at 9:30 pm en trained at Woolwich at 11.15 pm. Last section left 9.15 am m.s. Embarked Southampton - sailed at 2.30 pm	2wa
SOUTHAMPTON	5			2wa
HAVRE	6	7 am	arrives + disembarks at HAVRE.	2wa
	7	4 pm	First section entrained at 4 pm. for the front next section at 3 am following morning	2wa
BERGUETTE & HAMIT BILLET	8		units detrained at BERGUETTE and safely billeted at HAMIT BILLET by 10 am. Immediately on disentraining No 1 section proceeded & attached itself temporarily to Lahore D A C at CALONNE supplying ammunition	2wa 2wa
	9		rest at Billet - cleaning harness, overhauling equipment wagons - Guns and Limbers	2wa
ROBECQ	10	6.30 pm	Instructions from C.R.A. to remove to ROBECQ 3 miles distant arrived + quartered 10 pm	2wa
	11 & 13		Still at Billet. No 1 section rejoins Column on 13th. No 3 Section proceeds and attaches temporarily to Lahore D A C at CALONNE supplying ammunition	2wa
	14	1.30 pm	Instructions to move at 4.30 pm but cancelled at 8.30 am following morning, and move at 6 Billets 7 pm.	2wa
PADRELLES	15-16		PADRELLES Heavy Roads much rain arrived at 6.49" West Reberg D.A.C. at BAC ST. MAUR. No IV Section proceeds & attaches temporarily & 6.49" West Reberg D.A.C. at BAC ST. MAUR. Still at Billet. General Routine. Received instructions at 6pm to move at 4 AM following morning	2wa
LA BORGUE	19	4 am	Unit moves off and contacts at LA BORGUE by 10 am Kairo	2wa
PARADIS	20	8 pm	marches off all billets arrived Billet PARADIS 8 pm Mont Kairo	2wa
	21-26		Still at Billet. General Routine. Rec'd orders at 4 pm to move to new Billet at 6.30 following morning	2wa
	24	5 pm		2wa
CORNET MALO	27	6.30 am	No II Section rejoins Column daily to Ridge amm. Col. morning. arrived new Billet CORNET MALO	2wa 2wa
	28-30		Still at Billet. General Routine. Drill Rifle Inspection. Servicing Horses - supplying ammn No IV Section rejoins Column	2wa 2wa
CARVIN	31		Rec'd orders at 10 am to move to new Billet at CARVIN - arrives at 7.30 pm.	2wa

1577 Wt. W10791/1773 500,000 1/15 D. D. & L. A.D.S.S./Forms/C. 2118.

WAR DIARY
INTELLIGENCE SUMMARY.
(Erase heading not required.)

Army Form C. 2118.

51st High Divisional Amm. Col.

Place	Date	Hour	Summary of Events and Information	Remarks and references to Appendices
ESTAIRS	July 1915 1-9		Still at Billet. Daily routine. Physical Drill, Exercising horses, mules, marching & Rifle drill & instruction, map reading. Lectures. Route marching. Bathing Parades. Supply of ammunition daily to Bdys. Amm. Cols.	nwa.
	10	10 am	Inches known to new Billet west of ESTAIRS. Marches off at 4pm — arrived at new Billet 6 pm.	nwa.
	11-24		At Billet with daily routine as above	nwa.
	25	11 am	Headquarters Divisional Artillery established at our Billet with O.C. assist acting C.R.A. Time table of By's move South received. Prepn orders for mobilisation issued for move.	nwa.
	26-27		Preparations for move — numbering horses, wagons, equipment, supply of amm. to Bdys, templates completed, installment, travel pass	nwa.
	28	7.30 am	First section moves off for entraining at LA GORGUE } 5 trains in all	nwa.
		11 pm	Last section " " " at LA GORGUE }	nwa.
	29	2 am	First section arrives & detrains at CORBIE moved into new Billet at	nwa.
		5 pm	Last section arrives and detrains at CORBIE moved into new billet at BUSSY LES DAOURS.	nwa.
BUSSY LES DAOURS	30		BUSSY LES DAOURS. At Billet daily Routine	nwa.
	31		At Billet daily Routine. Supply of ammunition to Bdys Amm. Cols.	nwa.

121/7333

51st Dist: Ammn Colln
Vol II
Aug Sep 1 + Oct 15

Army Form C. 2118.

WAR DIARY
INTELLIGENCE SUMMARY.
(Erase heading not required.)

51st (High) Divisional Ammun Col
R.F.A.

Instructions regarding War Diaries and Intelligence Summaries are contained in F. S. Regs., Part II. and the Staff Manual respectively. Title pages will be prepared in manuscript.

Place	Date	Hour	Summary of Events and Information	Remarks and references to Appendices
	August 1915			
BUSSY LES DAOURS.	1		At Billet - daily routine - Marching & Rifle drill - instruction - Ammn. supply to Divs Ammn Colo.	Ewa
	4		At Billet - daily routine - new V.O. LIEUT. C.E.W. BRYAN arrives - Ammn supply to units	Ewa
	5		at Billet - daily routine - at 1.10 p.m. orders received from 51st Divn for moving	Ewa
	6		at Billet - daily routine - left Billet at 9 pm - arrived at new Billet BAVELIN	Ewa
	7	6 pm	Preparations for move - left Billet at 9 pm - arrived at new Billet BAVELIN COURT at 12 nom.	Ewa
BAVELIN COURT	8		At Billet - daily routine - Marching & Rifle drill - riding classes - lectures - short route marches - movements. Ammn supply.	Ewa
	15			
	16		Visit from Lieuts R.A. Allison & O. F.O.C. 51st Divn. Staff - inspection of encampment. Ammn supply.	Ewa
	17		at Billet - daily routine - Ammn supply - mode cutting party (50) detailed from unit to assist in setting trenches for trench rr. movement.	Ewa
	29			
	30		At Billet - Divisl Art.y having been supplies with 18 pr guns - all wagons set out 30/31 drawing new Ammn from Railhead FLESSELLES returning for supply of 16 wagon lines - also collecting taking back to Railhead 15 pr Ammn. All new 18 pr Ammn drawn during the night.	Ewa
	31			
			Weather on whole fine - from 12th to 25th showery changeable - During the month all spare linen teams were employed in harvesting operations - gathering in of the crops.	Ewa

WAR DIARY
INTELLIGENCE SUMMARY
(Erase heading not required.)

Army Form C. 2118.

51st (High.) Division A. Amm. Col. R.F.A.

Place	Date	Hour	Summary of Events and Information	Remarks and references to Appendices
Sept 1915				
BAVELIN COURT	1		Completing return "5" amm. Completing the filling up of the Ridge Amm Cols. with new 15th Amm.	Zuva
" "	2 to 15		Daily routine – amm. supply.	Zuva
" "			At Billet – on receipt of orders to prepare in into quarto, looking out suitable horse lines billets.	Zuva
" "	7		At Billet Lieut T. JENKINS of this Unit proto to 1st High F.A. Bde.	Zuva
" "	16		At Billet – conversation with mayor of village on purposes also rates regarding reception of divisional trains, also views to obtaining same for billets. Making arrangements, reporting thereon. Also surveying roads supply of districts reporting thereon. Amm. supply	Zuva
" "	17		At Billet – enquiries & preparations & visits quarto for various horse roads houses billettes to the different sections.	Zuva
" "	to		Wood cutting tanks of 30 men & wagons details to assist forestis detachment in cutting timber for trench stables. Erecting stables & repairing billets. Amm. supply.	Zuva
" "	30		Weather on whole fine & warm. Harvesting operations continues during the month. Crops thereof in order to clear out barns to be available for billetting the troops.	Zuva

Army Form C. 2118.

WAR DIARY
or
INTELLIGENCE SUMMARY. 51st (Highl) Divisional Amm. Col.
R.F.A.

(Erase heading not required.)

Instructions regarding War Diaries and Intelligence Summaries are contained in F. S. Regs., Part II. and the Staff Manual respectively. Title pages will be prepared in manuscript.

Place	Date	Hour	Summary of Events and Information	Remarks and references to Appendices
BAVELIN COURT	October 1915			
	1		at Billet - erecting stables & preparing billets. Hueshing of crops completed about 10th. Barns cleared out taken over for the troops. Wool cutting party still on duty. Loan of 15 wagons to various units to assist in carting turnips &c to stables & billets. Ammn supply daily.	Eura
	6 30			
	25		Billets completed. Roll men under Coor Parades with buses.	Eura
	4		Lieut F. E. Davis from 1st Corps Amm Park attached to Unit.	Eura
			Inspection of Unit by Major General J. M. Harfer C.B. D.S.O. and P.O.C. of 51st Division	Eura
	9		Visit of Major General Beare C.R.A. X Corps.	Eura
	12		Visit of Lieut General Sir T. L. N. Morland G.O.C. 10 Corps	Eura
	21		Weather for first 3 weeks good - chilly at night. Last week wet & cold.	Eura

121/7636

ڃ ٣

حصہ ١

محررہ ٢٥،١،٥

پنڈی سوسٹ صیغہ

٥١ تا

Army Form C. 2118.

51st (High) Divisional
Ammn. Col. R.F.A. (7)

WAR DIARY
or
INTELLIGENCE SUMMARY.
(Erase heading not required.)

Instructions regarding War Diaries and Intelligence Summaries are contained in F. S. Regs., Part II. and the Staff Manual respectively. Title pages will be prepared in manuscript.

Places	Date	Hour	Summary of Events and Information	Remarks and references to Appendices
BAVELIN COURT	November 1915			
	1 to 30		Still at Billets - General Routine - Daily Ammunition Supply to Bdys. Ammn. Cols & driers units - Completing erection of stables - all stables completed about 17th of month. - making roads into hopples around stables. - Supply of wagons to C.R.E. for fabricating timber to front area two 5 cutters parties furnished.	
	11	9 am.	Half of 7 A. Bdy leaving joined 51st (High) Division, a section of Lowland's D.A.C. joined this unit with 2 off. 104 O.R. 126 mules 14 horses + 21 wagons - all billets same day.	ENWA
	12		Drawing rations for the establishment of 18 pr Ammn. to Lowland's half of Ammn. Col. & D.A.C. Section	ENWA
	23	5 pm.	1/11" London (How) Battery R.F.A. having joined 51st (Hyd)Dis 1 off. 15 O.R. 22 horses + 3 wagons joined this unit with 4.5" ammn + all Billets line.	ENWA
	30		Visit of General Eddee Commanding R.A. X Corps - Heavy fall of snow on 15th + 16 x Carlo.	ENWA
			Weather for first part of month good. - Heavy fall of snow on 15th + 16th - weather good from 20th to 27th - frost keen on 28 - 29 & 30. Very wet snow	ENWA

F. M. Alexander Capt.
Adjt: 51st Highland Divisional Ammn. Colmn. R.F.A.

51st Ind. Arrow. Co.

Age
vol. VI

Army Form C. 2118.

WAR DIARY
INTELLIGENCE SUMMARY.
(Erase heading not required.)

51st Divl. Ammn. Col. R.F.A.

Place	Date	Hour	Summary of Events and Information	Remarks and references to Appendices
BAVELIN COURT	1915			
	1st 6th 31st		At Billet. General Routine – supply of Ammunition daily to Bdge Ammn Columns – Refreshing drill – Lectures &c	Ywar.
	5		Lub. section 10th D.A.C. – one officer 19 O.R. 21 horses & 3 wagons – returns to own Unit	Ywa.
	17 21		Lowland D.A.C. section strength 2 offs + 104 O.R. 19 wagons, 126 mules & 10 horses absorbed into establishment of this Unit	Ywa. Ywa.
	15 20		one officer + 6 O.R. attached from 32nd D.A.C. for instruction. Party of 1 officer + 40 D.R. attached from 32nd Divl. Artillery as wood cutting party	Ywa.
	23		officer + 6 O.R. from 31st D.A.C. returns to his Unit	Ywa.
	24		Wood cutting party returned to his Unit.	Ywa.
	27 5 29		Inoculation of horses & mules by A.D.V.S. for test for glanders	Ywa. Ywa.
			Weather wet & cold. Strong for first fort of month. clears turnpiene's towards end of month – snow on 11th	
			Gas sharp.	Kodo Capt r Adjt

T. v. Averingt. Lt. Col.
Commanding Highland Divisional Ammn. Column.

51 High Div Amm Col
Jan 1916
Vol V

Army Form C. 2118

WAR DIARY
or
INTELLIGENCE SUMMARY
(Erase heading not required.)

51st (Highland) Divisional Amm Col R.F.A.

Adjt: 51st Highland Divisional Ammn Comn. R.F.A.
Capt. T. Alexander
Col R.F.A.

Place	Date	Hour	Summary of Events and Information	Remarks and references to Appendices
BAVEL- INCOURT	January 1916 1/2 3		Still at Billet - Ammunition supply - preparations for move to back area - Instructions recvd that Column to be organised into 3 Section Column - absorbing no 4 section among sections 1, 2 & 3.	Pera
	4		Sections 2 & 3 left at 9 am. for new area - arrives at ARGOEUVES about 3 pm. Still at Billet.	Pera
	5		Headqrs and 5 Section no 1 still at Billet - Ammunition supply - making arrangements to hand over to relieving unit - 30. D.A.C. Sections 1 & 3 of 30. D.A.C. arrives with party of officers on tour of instruction - Visit of A.Q.M.G. 51st Div. with parties of officers on tour of instruction - Lecture on organisation of D.A.C., methods of supply & admin. carried out.	Pera
	6 & 7		Ammunition supply - preparing for move of remainder of Column.	Pera
	8		Headqrs no 1 Section left Billet for ARGOEUVES at 9 am arrives there about 3 pm.	Pera
ARGOE UVES	9/16 31st		At Billet - assisting in building & horse standings for Div. Coln; repair ing billet - overhauling equipment & reorganising - drawing and issuing 4.5 Hrs ammn. for 3 High (Hors) Bdge. new equipped with 4.5 Hows returning oes 5" Ammn - supply & ammn to other Bdges to fill up to establishment. Divisional Portable store established where D.A.C. - Drawing stores and filling up to the store. Refitting still - regrading classes. Returns re ammn stated by C.R.A.	Pera
	31		Weather for first week cold showery - for remainder of month very good - dry - little rain.	Pera

Army Form C. 2118

WAR DIARY
or
INTELLIGENCE SUMMARY
(Erase heading not required.)

51st (Highland) Divisional Amm. Col

Instructions regarding War Diaries and Intelligence Summaries are contained in F.S. Regs., Part II. and the Staff Manual respectively. Title Pages will be prepared in manuscript.

Place	Date	Hour	Summary of Events and Information	Remarks and references to Appendices
BAVEL INCOURT	January 1916 1/6 3		Still at Billet. Ammunition supply. Preparations for move to back area. Instructions received that Column to be organised as a 3 Section Column absorbing No 4 section among sections 1, 2 & 3.	Mem.
	4		Sections 2 & 3 left at 9 a.m. for new area arrived at ARGOEUVES about 3 p.m. Billets made.	Cwa
	5		Headqrs and 5 Section No 1 still at Billet. Ammunition supply making arrangements to hand over to relieving unit 30° D.A.C. arrived.	Cwa
	6 & 7		Sections 1 & 3 of 30° D.A.C. with party of officers on tour instruction visit of A.A.Q.M.G. 51st Div. matters supply & admm. carried - lectures on organisation of D.A.C.	Alexander Cwa
	6 & 7		Ammn. supply. Preparing for move & remainder of Column.	Cwa
	8		Headqrs & No 1 Section left Billets for ARGOEUVES at 9 a.m. arrived there about 3 p.m.	Cwa
ARGOEUVES	9/6 31st		at Billet - according to instructions from lower standing for Dis Amty repairing billets - overhauling equipment & re-org. drawing and cleaning 4.5 How. Ammn. for 3° High. (Hons) Brigde road supplies Butt & 5 guns to returning old 5" Ammn. supply & Ammn. to new Bde to fill up to establishment. Divisional Stable store established after D.A.C. - drawing grenades and filling returns etc. Refreshing drill - signalling classes - lectures to C.R.A. inspection of unit - Horse motto's to C.R.A.	Cwa
	31		Weather for first week cold, thawing & much very soft - latterly remainder of month very good - dry - little rain	Cwa

WAR DIARY or INTELLIGENCE SUMMARY

Army Form C. 2118

51st (Highland) Divisional Ammn Col R.F.A.

Place	Date	Hour	Summary of Events and Information	Remarks and references to Appendices
BAVELINCOURT	January 1916 1 2 3		Still at Billet - Ammunition supply - Preparations for move to back area. Instructions received. Col to reconnoitre a shelter. Column absorbing No 4 section ammunition columns 1, 2 & 3.	Bra
	4		Sections 2 & 3 left at 9 am for new area arrives at ARGOEUVES about 3 pm Utilise rails.	Guide
	5		Hoofs and no 5 section no 1 still at Billet - Ammunition supply making arrangements to hand over to relieving unit - 30 S.A.C. Sections 1 & 3 & JO' D.A.C. ammn S. Visit of A. A. Q.M.G. 51 Div. with party of officers on tour of instruction. Lecture on ammunition. O A C. notes supply, return carried.	Two ao
	6 & 7		Ammn supply preparing for move to ammunition Column.	
	8		Hoofs and No 1 section left Billet for ARGOEUVES at 9 am arrives about 3 pm.	
ARGOEUVES	9 10		At Billet - according to instructions from standing for 3rd H.C.F. hrs Bdge refresh ammn Billets - overhauling equipment & reorganising - drawing and cleaning 4-5 How Ammn for 3" H.y.E. hrs Bdge now equipped. Build 4-5 amm to returning old SA Ammn to other Bdges & fill up to establishment. Ammn supply x Ammn to our Bdges. Division ammunition Dum. minimal flexible stay established against O.A.C. Ammn parades and filling up the stores. Reports still - signalling lamps Returns to C.R.A. - twice posted. Weather for first week cold showery - for remainder of month very cold - dry - little rain	Bug Bug

Army Form C. 2118.

WAR DIARY
or
INTELLIGENCE SUMMARY.
(Erase heading not required.)

51st DIVL. AMMN. COL. RFA

Place	Date	Hour	Summary of Events and Information	Remarks and references to Appendices
ARGOEUVES	FEBRUARY.			
	1-5		Generally overhauling, cleaning wagons, harness, equipment, kit. Reporting from 3rd line unit reported for duty.	
	2		Kit Armstrong reported for duty. (Hon Lieut.) (from woodcutting duty.)	
	5		Kit Palmeroy posted 51/1 Lowlands Fd. Bde. from this date.	
	6-7		Preparation began for move to new camp.	
	8		The column moved from ARGOEUVES to SAILLY LE SEC	
SAILLY LE SEC	9		Cleaning of billets which are in a very unhealthy state.	
	10		Inspection of lines by Brigade Major & Capt Captain.	
	11-19		General routine. Cleaning of horses & lines. Very bad weather.	
	13		Colonel Robertson attends Course of instruction at BEAUVAL for 8 days.	
	19		Capt Weemele assumes temporary command of unit.	
	21		Colonel Robertson resumes command of unit on return from Course.	
	27		Very heavy fall of snow. Transport very difficult. Orders to move to CHIPILLY received but cancelled about 12 midnight. Standing fast awaiting further orders.	
VILLERS-BOCAGE	29		Left SAILLY LE SEC at 11.30 am for VILLERS-BOCAGE arriving at 9 pm. Very long trek.	

Army Form C. 2118.

WAR DIARY
or
INTELLIGENCE SUMMARY.
(Erase heading not required.)

51st DIVL AMMN. COL. RFA

Place	Date	Hour	Summary of Events and Information	Remarks and references to Appendices
	March			
VILLERS-BOCAGE	1		Sorting out of lines and preparing for further moves.	JB
	3		Visit from C.R.A. Very heavy fall of snow.	JB
	6		Column left VILLERS-BOCAGE at 10.30 a.m. for HEM arriving there at 4 p.m. Colonel Robertson assumed temporary command of 51st Divl. Arty. during the absence of C.R.A.	JB
	8		No 3 Section moves from HEM to REBREUVES. Capt Life and 11 men are detailed to form Ammn. dump at ANZIN ST AUBIN in forwards area.	JB
REBREUVES	9.		Remainder of Column move to REBREUVES. 2 NCOs & men detached to 3rd Army Trench Mortar School.	JB
	10		Orders to Column to move to BERLANCOURT received at mid-day but cancelled at 4 p.m. owing to scarcity of billets there. No 3 Section move forward to HABARCQ. Lieut Blan- nch & 6 men attached to form Ammn. dump at MAROEUIL in forward area.	JB
BERLANCOURT	11		left REBREUVES for BERLANCOURT at 10 a.m. Visit from A.A. + Q.M.G. 51st Division	JB
Bois d'HABARCQ	14.		moved to Bois d'HABARCQ	JB

Army Form C. 2118.

WAR DIARY
or
INTELLIGENCE SUMMARY.
(Erase heading not required.)

51.(HIGH) DIVL AMM COL

Place	Date	Hour	Summary of Events and Information	Remarks and references to Appendices
	MARCH			
TILLOY	15		Column moved from BOIS D'IHAB ARCQ. to TILLOY No 3 Section rejoined Column here.	
BERLES	16		Column marched to BERLES. Good billets.	
	17-31		Still at BERLES. General Routine. Daily supply of Ammunition to Bde Columns etc.	
	21		Capt. Collis transferred to Adv'ce R.F.C. late attached as observer	
	23		Bad weather. Very heavy fall of snow	
	26		Visit from OC 10th Corps Ammn Park.	
	28		Change in the weather conditions. Very much improved	
	31		Visit from AA. & QMG. 51st Division. Staff Capt 51st Div Art. & ADVS. Situation of 28th DAC attached to the Column, 6 offrs. 117th Bde of Artillery, attached to 51st Division. 1 officer, 41 OR. +3 horses + 6 mules.	

John Oliver Hind
Lt. Col.
for Commanding Highland Divisional Ammn. Colmn.

WAR DIARY or INTELLIGENCE SUMMARY

Army Form C. 2118

High Div. Amn. Col. Vol 8

Place	Date	Hour	Summary of Events and Information	Remarks and references to Appendices
MONCHEL	April 1.	4 p.m.	Still in Billet. Headquarters:- SHEET 51C, N.E. D.9.c central.	
BERLES.	2-6th		Bil. section. 25th D.A.C. attached to 51st D.A.C. Reported under Lieut. A. WISE.	
			Daily Routine. Normal supply of Ammunition to Brigade Columns daily.	
	7th	12 noon	127 other ranks reinforcements, received from 3rd Line.	
	8th	2 p.m.	do. do. 51st Divl. Infantry Base Depot.	
	9-15th		Daily Routine. Normal supply of Ammunition to Brigade Columns daily.	
	16th		Captain R.B. FIFE completes Bourse of Instruction at Third Army School of Mortars, and appointed Trench Mortar Officer for the 51st Division. Struck off strength of 51st D.A.C. accordingly. 281 Sergt. A REID promoted 2nd Lieut. and posted to 51st D.A.C.	
			Daily Routine. Lectures on Discipline, Standing Orders, by O.C. to reinforcements.	
	17-18		2nd Lieut. R.E. REID posted to 51st D.A.C. from 2nd Lowland Brigade R.F.A.	
	19th		Lecture on "GAS" by O.C. to reinforcements.	
			Daily Routine. Supply of Ammunition to Brigade Columns normal.	
	20-24		Lectures to reinforcements on Horse and Mule management by Capt. SMITH, O.C. No. 3 Section.	
	25th	10 a.m.	Bil. section of 25th D.A.C. instructed to rejoin their Unit on 27th inst.	
	26th		Visit from C.O.C. Third Army, and Major General JOHNSTON.	
	27th		Bil. section of 25th D.A.C. rejoined their Unit at VILLERS-BRULIN.	
	28-29th		Daily Routine. Normal supply of ammunition to Brigade Amm. Colo.	
			Weather very good throughout the month.	
	29th + 30th		Lecture on organisation of D.A.C.; System of supply of ammunition, and on the various kinds of ammunition carried and handled by the Column (by O.C.)	

Jas. M. Fulton Dunn Capt.
for Lt. Col.
Commanding Highland Divisional Ammn. Colmn.

WAR DIARY
INTELLIGENCE SUMMARY
(Erase heading not required.)

Army Form C. 2118

51D Amm Col Vol 9

Place	Date	Hour	Summary of Events and Information	Remarks and references to Appendices
MONCHEL BERLES.	May 7.7.		In Billet. Headquarters, Sheet 51c N.E. D9.c central. Daily routine. Ammunition supply to Brigade Amm.Cols. daily.	
	8th		Inspection of Lines by General HENSHAW. Very favourable report received.	
	9.14		Daily Routine. Daily Ammunition supply. Unsettled weather. Roads heavy.	
	15th	10 am	Instructions received regarding the Reorganization of the D.A.C.	
	16th		Preparation for billeting of 1st, 2nd & 3rd Highland, and 1st Lowland Brigade Amm.Cols.	
	17th	Noon	1st, 2nd & 3rd Highland and 1st Lowland Brigade Ammn.Cols. joined 51st D.A.C. and were absorbed in strength of D.A.C.	
	19th		Reorganization being completed.	
	21st		100 Remounts received from 5th Division.	Appendix No.1 recvd 15/5/16.
	25th	10 am	Instructions received for Nos.1, 2 & 3 Sections to move out to new Billets. Situation SHEET 51c N.E., No.1 = E.10 central, No.2 = K.11.f central, No.3 = E.22.d. central.	
	26th		78 Remounts received from 25th Divisional Artillery.	
	28th		Abnormal supply of Gun Ammunition to Brigade Columns to complete new establishment. New Ammunition Refilling Point :- Situation 51c N.E. E.29.b central.	
	29th		Lt. Col. C McLEOD ROBERTSON, commanding 51st D.A.C., assumes command (temporarily) of 51st Divisional Artillery. Captain MITCHELL INNES, O.C. No.3 Section D.A.C. assumes command of 51st D.A.C. vice Lt. Col. C. McLEOD ROBERTSON.	
	31st		Inspection of Lines by C.R.A., 51st Division.	

W. McIntosh Lun Lt. Col.
Commanding Highland Divisional Ammn.Colmn.

With War Diary for MAY, 1916

Appendices No. 1.

Re - organization of the system of ammunition

supply within the Division -

In order to meet the changed conditions consequent on the growth of the Army, and to provide an organization which will be more manageable and more economical than that at present existing, the Commander - in - Chief has decided -

(A) to abolish the Brigade Ammunition Columns as such;

(B) to re - constitute the Divisional Ammunition Columns into Divisional Columns, of two echelons each, composed as follows :-

Headquarters,

" A " Echelon, consisting of three sections
             (Nos: 1, 2 and 3 Sections)
"B" Echelon, consisting of 1 section
             (No: 4 Section).

The Headquarters and " A " echelon are designed to accompany the Division closely at all times.

" B " echelon will follow the Division if circumstances permit, but is detachable under Corps control when necessary.

....

This re - organization will be commenced forthwith, the surplus personnel, horses and vehicles, being disposed of under orders to be issued by the Adjutant General and Quartermaster General.

(Signed) R. BUTLER.
                                                    M.G.
General Headquarters,   for Lieutenant - General,
6th May, 1916.   C. G. S.

WAR DIARY
or
INTELLIGENCE SUMMARY.
(Erase heading not required.)

Army Form C. 2118.

Vol 10

Place	Date	Hour	Summary of Events and Information	Remarks and references to Appendices
MONCHEL BERLES.	JUNE 1st to 6th		In Billet. Headquarters - Sheet 51c N.E. D.9.c central	
	7th		Notification received of loss of H.M.S. "HAMPSHIRE" with LORD KITCHENER and Staff.	
	8th	9 a.m.	Instructions issued No.2 Section to move from LARESSET [Sheet 51c N.E. E.11.2 central] to CAPELLE - FERMONT [E.8 central] [same reference Sheet].	
	9th		Lt. Col. C. McL. ROBERTSON resumed command of unit on the return of the C.R.A.	
	10th	6 p.m.	Instructions received for Headquarters and No.4 Section to move from MONCHEL-BERLES to AGNIERES [Sheet 51c N.E. E.2.2 central] on the 12th June.	
	11th		Preparations for move.	
	12th	10 a.m.	Headquarters and No.4 Section moved off for new billet, arriving 12.30 p.m.	
AGNIERES	13th-14th		Settling down in new billet. Naval Ammunition Supply.	
	15th	7 p.m.	Lorry, one other route, supernumerary to establishment, sent to Base Depot.	
	16th	9 a.m.	Three officers - Lt. McBAIN F and Lts. SINCLAIR and ANDERSON, with eighty one other ranks transferred to 220 mm. French Siege Gun, attached to 11th Liege Battery R.G.A.	
	17th		Visit from Lt. Col. MOIR. P.S.O. Int.	
	18th-27th		Abnormal demands for Ammunition from F.A. Base.	
	28th		Issue of Gun Ammunition stopped by XVII Corps Ammunition, on Authority of XVII Corps.	

Army Form C. 2118.

WAR DIARY
or
INTELLIGENCE SUMMARY.
(Erase heading not required.)

Instructions regarding War Diaries and Intelligence Summaries are contained in F. S. Regs., Part II. and the Staff Manual respectively. Title pages will be prepared in manuscript.

Place	Date	Hour	Summary of Events and Information	Remarks and references to Appendices
AGNIERES	JUNE 29th. 30th.		No. 3 Section moves from HAUTE AVESNES to join Headquarters at AGNIERES. Issue of Ammunition being made from establishment in view of XVII Corps Instructions. 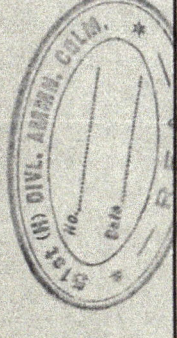 J. N. Alexander Capt & Adjt for Lt. Col. Commanding 51st D.A.C.	

Confidential

No 309/A
HIGHLAND
DIVISION

XI

War Diary

57th Divl. Ammunition Column

from 1st July 1916 to 31st July 1916

Volume I

Army Form C. 2118

WAR DIARY
INTELLIGENCE SUMMARY
(Erase heading not required.)

Instructions regarding War Diaries and Intelligence Summaries are contained in F.S. Regs., Part II. and the Staff Manual respectively. Title Pages will be prepared in manuscript.

Place	Date	Hour	Summary of Events and Information	Remarks and references to Appendices
AGNIERES	July 1st		In Billets. Headquarters. Sheet 51 C.N.E. D.G.C. central. Weather dull. Ammunition supply normal.	swra
	2		Batteries of 60th Division which came up into position on 1st & 2nd drawing ammunition from 51st D.A.C. Abnormal supply which taxes the resources of the Column.	swra
	3		Ammunition supply again normal. Wet weather.	swra
	4		Ammunition supply still normal. 5 officers of 60th D.A.C. (O.C., Adjt. & 3 other officers) attached to 51 D.A.C. for instruction in ammunition supply.	swra
	5			swra
	6-13		Fatigue. R.E. Services. Weather warm.	swra
	14	6 p.m.	Operation Orders received from Headquarters, Divisional Artillery. Column to move to new area at 7 a.m. on 15th. Men on fatigue duties recalled. Party of officers and men attached 11th Siege Battery returned to unit. Busy packing up and generally arranging departure.	swra
	15	7 a.m.	Left Agnières. Proceeds with Divisional Artillery via Haute Avesnes and Habarcq to LUCHEUX (SHEET ———). Scorching day. Arrives LUCHEUX at 2.30 p.m.	swra
	16	4.30 a.m.	Operation Orders received. Column to move with Divisional Artillery to BOISBERGUES (———). Left LUCHEUX at 9.30 a.m. Arrives BOISBERGUES at 7.30 p.m. Inspected by C.R.A. en route.	swra
	17	3 p.m.	Operation Order received, also a special order referring to operations to be carried out by the Division in the near future. Order cancelling move received at 6 p.m.	swra
	18		Captain BRYAN A.V.C. transferred from attached duties with D.A.C. to 2nd Veterinary Hospital ABBEVILLE. Succeeded by Lt. HANNA who is attached to 260th Bde. R.F.A.	swra
	19	4 p.m.	Operation Order received. Column to proceed to new area at VIGNACOURT (———). Column moves off at 6 p.m. Hot afternoon & beautiful moonlit night.	swra
	20	4 p.m.	Operation order cancelling Column to move to DERNANCOURT (ALBERT combines sheet E. 20.C. central). Moved at 6.30 p.m.	swra

1875 Wt. W593/826 1,000,000 4/15 J.B.C. & A. A.D.S.S./Forms/C. 2118.

WAR DIARY

INTELLIGENCE SUMMARY

(Erase heading not required.)

Army Form C. 2118

Place	Date	Hour	Summary of Events and Information	Remarks and references to Appendices
	July 20	3.30am	Arrived at area outside DERNANCOURT (a tremendous file covers with troops). No billets. Lines under tarpaulins.	Sws.
	22		1 Officer & 6 O.R. proceeded to Dump at MAMETZ WOOD (S.13. D.a.u. ALBERT Conibinit sheet) to take over Grenade and T.M. ammunition Dump from 33rd D.A.C. 1 Officer & party took over Gun ammunition Dump at FRICOURT (ALBERT Combinet, F.9.c.9.1.) from 21st D.A.C.	Sws.
	23		All gun ammunition dumped by D.A.C. at FRICOURT Dump during night 22nd – 23rd.	Sws.
	24	2 pm	Operation Order received. Column moves to new area at 2 pm. Arrived at area 3 pm. Encamped at VIVIER MILL (SHEET 62.D.N.E. Edition 2. E.16.a central). Abnormal issue of ammunition.	Sws.
	25	12.30pm	Order received for 1 Officer & 99 O.R. to dig in wire at 258th Bde R.F.A. Information received at 4 pm. that several of the party has been wounded. Total casualties 1 Died of wounds. 8 wounded.	Sws.
	26	4 am	Urgent demand from 258 Bde R.F.A. for 150 gas helmets, the Brigade having been under gas attack for seven hours. 150 helmets got from Divisions and sent up at once.	Sws.
	27		Warm weather. Abnormal amm. supply from Dump.	Sws.
	28		20 O.R. posted to D/160 Bty. R.F.A. to replace casualties.	Sws.
	29		Dump at ROSE COTTAGE, FRICOURT removed to BECORDEL (ALBERT Combinet. F.7. central).	Sws.
	30		Weather cold & tropical.	Sws.
	31		Captain F. SMITH slightly wounded while on duty in forward area. Abnormal supply of ammunition from 22nd. to end of month. Weather excellent during month, except first week, which was wet. Latter part of month extremely hot.	Sws.

Charles Webster, Lt.Col.
51st D.A.C.

51st Divisional Artillery.

51st DIVISIONAL AMMUNITION COLUMN R.F.A.

::::::AUGUST 1 9 1 6::::

WAR DIARY
or
INTELLIGENCE SUMMARY 51st (Highland) Divisional Ammunition Column R.F.A.

Army Form C. 2118

No 21 (7)
HIGHLAND

(Erase heading not required.)

Place	Date	Hour	Summary of Events and Information	Remarks and references to Appendices
MÉAULTE	August 1		In Billets. Abnormal ammunition supply. 3 teams went up late at night to bring back 3 captured guns from forward area.	
	2	9.30am	2 guns taken into line. Remaining one has to be fixed with wheels. Team went up in evening to bring it back.	
	3	6.30am	Remaining gun brought into D.A.C. lines.	
	4	2pm	3 captured guns taken to D.D.O.S. Fourth Army. Heavy ammunition supply.	
	5-6		Heavy ammunition supply.	
	7	5.30pm	H.Q. and reinforcements arrived from Base Depot and allotted to Sections.	
	8		Ammunition supply heavy. Personnel of Medium T.M. Batteries attached to D.A.C. prior to move.	
	9		Heavy ammunition supply.	
	10	6pm	Operation Order No. 43 received. Column to move at 10.10 a.m. on 11th. Preparations for move.	
	11	10.10am	Column proceeded via DERNANCOURT, BUIRE, RIBEMONT, HEILLY, to BONNAY (Amiens 17; G.1.22). Bivouacs in Park.	
	12	4pm	Operation Order No. 44 received. Preparations for move.	
	13		Sections 1, 2 & 3 moved to entraining point at LONGUEAU Station (Amiens 17, E.2.26) and SALEUX Station (Amiens 17, C.29.3) and in 4 portions along with sections of 78 and starting from BONNAY at 1.30 p.m. Sections 1 & 2 entrained at LONGUEAU Station. Section 3. at SALEUX Station. First train left 8.58 pm.	
	14	8.26am	Last train of Sections 1, 2, 3 left SALEUX. Headquarters Section 4 entrained in portions. Headquarters at SALEUX Station. 10th at both stations. Last train left LONGUEAU at 2.58 pm	
	15		D.A.C. detrained, partly at STEENBECQUE (HAZEBROUCK 5A. F.47.1) and partly at ARQUES (D.45.8). and concentrated at LYNDE (F.4.0.6) last wagons coming in at 4 a.m. Operation Order No. 45 received at 4 pm.	
	16		T.M. Personnel left at 2 p.m. for front. Advance party proceeded to new area to reconnoitre and to take over 2 ammunition dumps.	
	17		Left LYNDE H.45 a.m. and proceeded via STEENBECQUE, ESTAIRES to area at PONT DE NIEPPE (Sheet 36, B.23 central) Sections apart. Arrived at 6 p.m. and relieved N.Z. D.A.C. Gun and T.M. Amn. Dumps at GARE ANNEXE (Sheet 36 B.30 & 2.3.8). Grenade dump at PLACE VICTOR HUGO (I.1.8.8.8.) taken over.	
	18-20		Ammunition supply to dumps.	

Army Form C. 2118

WAR DIARY
INTELLIGENCE SUMMARY
(Erase heading not required.)

Instructions regarding War Diaries and Intelligence Summaries are contained in F. S. Regs., Part II. and the Staff Manual respectively. Title Pages will be prepared in manuscript.

Place	Date	Hour	Summary of Events and Information	Remarks and references to Appendices
PONT-DE-NIEPPE.	August 21.	5am.	10. OR reinforcements arrives from Base Depôt and allots to Sections.	2WAR
	22.		200 ALTR received. Sections marined. 1 Officer (2/Lt. SINCLAIR DG.) 99 OR. attaches 51 V (Heavy) T.M. Battery for duty from Column.	2WAR
	23.		Major W.H. ANDERSON (Mach. Bde. RFA) appointed to command No. 1 Section DAC. Captain A.T. DAWSON (258 Bde. RFA) postes to H.Q. DAC. for duty.	2WAR
	24/27.		Usual returns. Normal Ammn. supply.	2WAR
	28.		Orders received for Headquarters Sections 1, 2 + 3 to move to new area round STEENWERCK.	2WAR
	29.		Headquarters Sections 1, 2 + 3 left old billets at 1 Am. Arrives at new billets 4pm. in deluge of rain. Headquarters at (Sheet 36. A.17. C.4.5). 2/Lieut. A.J.C. FYFE + 2/Lieut. A.B. HARPER transferred for duty to 39th Division. 2/Lieut. ANDERSON J.S. attaches 51 V. T.M. Bty.	2WAR
	30/31		Establishing communication with Battery wagon lines. Normal ammunition supplies to Divn to Aus. brigades.	2WAR
			First three weeks very warm and sunny. Latter part showery and changeable.	2WAR

J.W. Alexander
Capt & Adjt
for Lt. Colonel
Commanding 51 (H) D.A.C.

CONFIDENTIAL
No. 21/A.
HIGHLAND DIVISION.

Vol 13

War Diary

of

51st (Highland) Divisional Ammunition Column R.F.A.

for

September 1916.

Army Form C. 2118

WAR DIARY
INTELLIGENCE SUMMARY
(Erase heading not required.)

51st (Highland) Divisional Ammunition Column R.F.A.

Instructions regarding War Diaries and Intelligence Summaries are contained in F.S. Regs., Part II. and the Staff Manual respectively. Title Pages will be prepared in manuscript.

Place	Date	Hour	Summary of Events and Information	Remarks and references to Appendices
STEENWERCK	1916 Sept. 1.		In Billets. Headquarters at Sn.S.4 (Hazebrouck 5A). T.M. Amm. Dump at Kn.S.3. Grenade Dump at Kn.6.2. Headquarters wagon lines moved to more suitable quarters outside town. Normal amm. supply.	Power
	2.-3.		Normal ammunition supply.	
	4.	10 a.m.	Visit from C.R.A. and Staff Captain R.A.	
	5.		Grenade Dump shelled in afternoon. 2 men wounded.	
	6-7.		Normal ammunition supply.	
	8.	1 p.m.	40 remounts arrive for unit. Found to be in poor condition.	
			Normal ammunition supply.	
	9.		Normal ammunition supply.	
	10.	7 a.m.	2/Lieut. A. REID & 2/Lieut. A. ROBERTSON left unit for transfer to 24th Division.	
	11.		12 N.C.O.s. + artificers supernumerary to establishment of Brigade, posted to D.A.C. 4 reinforcements arrives from 5000 Depôt, 8 p.m.	
	12.-14.		Normal ammunition supply.	
	15.		Captain D. ANZON posted to D/255 Bde. R.F.A.	
	16.		Ammunition supply normal.	
	17.		Colonel ROBERTSON grants 10 days leave. Major ANDERSON, o.c. No.1 Section, assumes command of D.A.C. during absence of Colonel.	
	18-19		Normal ammunition supply.	
	20.		D.A.C. ordered to supply spring waggons running out to complete batteries to establishment with 1 spare of each.	
	21.	6 p.m.	Operation Order No. 147 received.	
	22.	9.30 a.m.	Collection of 101 remounts from Railhead for Division.	
	23.	2 p.m.	40 Remounts collected by D.A.C. and distributed among Sections.	
	24.	4.55 p.m.	Operation Order No. 148 received. Instructions for commencement of move to new area.	
	25.	7.15 a.m.	Left STEENWERCK and proceeds via ESTAIRES, MERVILLE, ROBECQ to BURBURE (F.6.75) where we arrives at 7 p.m.	
		7.30 p.m.	Operation Order No. BM.365 received.	
	26.	9.45 a.m.	Left BURBURE and proceeds via PERNES and TANGRY to ANVIN (D1.14. Sheet LENS II) and MONCHY-CAYEUX (D1.3.2) arrives at 3.15 p.m. Headquarters No 3 Section Billets in ANVIN; Sections 1, 2, 4 at MONCHY-CAYEUX. Operation Order No. BM. 271 received 8 p.m.	

Army Form C. 2118

WAR DIARY (continued)
INTELLIGENCE SUMMARY
(Erase heading not required.)

51st (Highland) Div. Amm. Col.

Place	Date	Hour	Summary of Events and Information	Remarks and references to Appendices
ANVIN	SEPTEMBER 27	10 a.m.	Left ANVIN and MONCHY-CAYEUX and proceeded via WAVRANS, CROISETTE, MONCHEL to CONCHY-SUR-CANCHE (C.3.4.6.) arriving there at 4 p.m. Operation Order No BM. 271 received 7.30 p.m.	2wwo
	28	9.30 am	Left CONCHY-SUR-CANCHE and proceeded via OCCOCHES + DOULLENS to LOUVENCOURT (G.5.1.2), arriving at 8 p.m. Operation Order No. BM 278 received at 9 p.m.	2wwo
	29	10.30 am	Left LOUVENCOURT and proceeded via RAINCHEVAL to PUCHEVILLERS (E.6.9.7), arriving at 1 p.m.	2wwo
	30	6 p.m.	Operation order No 449 received, for continuation of move on following day (1.10.16) to HEDAUVILLE	2wwo
			Weather favourable during month, with intervals of rain.	2wwo

T. W. Clemenson Capt. ra.g.t
for Lieut Colonel
Commanding 51st (High) Div. Amm. Col.
R.F.A.

CONFIDENTIAL.
No 21/A
HIGHLAND DIVISION.

Vol 14

War Diary.
of
51st (Highland) Divisional Ammunition Column R.F.A.
for
October, 1916.

Army Form C. 2118.

WAR DIARY
INTELLIGENCE SUMMARY.
(Erase heading not required.)

51st (Highland) Divisional Ammunition Column RFA

Place	Date	Hour	Summary of Events and Information	Remarks and references to Appendices
PUCHEVILLERS	October 1	1 p.m.	Moves via Toutencourt, Leavillers, Varennes to Hedauville. Headquarters established at (Sheet 57D V.14.b.49) Section 4 billeted at Varennes (P.32.a.27). 2 officers 49 other ranks of British West Indies Regiment attached for rations to DAC and for work at the Dump, packing empty cases etc.	SWA
	2	9 a.m.	High DAC handed over Ammunition Dump to 51st DAC. The Dump being almost empty of gun ammy. heavy demands were supplies out of DAC establishment	SWA
	3	3 a.m.	First allotment of ammunition deposited at Dump from Park. Section moves into field vacated by High DAC, at 11 a.m. Heavy ammunition supply to Brigades of 18th, 39th and 51st Divisions. Orders received at 4 p.m. from HQ Div Arty. to issue gun ammunition to 51st Division only.	SWA
	4	9 a.m.	S.A.A. Section of Section 2 proceeded to Louvencourt (1.35 central) under charge of 1 officer. Abnormal amm. supply from Dump. Section 4 moves at 10 a.m. from Varennes to Field at V.S.C. central. No billets	SWA
	5		Heavy ammunition supply.	SWA
	6	11 a.m.	Operation Order No 50 received DAC to move out full of ammunition. Echelons immediately filled out. Column proceeds at 1 p.m. via Forceville and Acheux to Louvencourt, where SAA Section rejoined it. No billets a number of tents and trench covers received on loan from Town Major. 1 officer (reinforcement) arrived and was posted to Section 3	SWA
	7	10 a.m.	Operation Order No 51 received. DAC not affected. Gun ammunition Dump established at Bus-les-Artois (J.19.d.9.7)	SWA

Army Form C. 2118.

WAR DIARY
of
INTELLIGENCE SUMMARY.
(Erase heading not required.)

51st (Highland) Divisional Ammunition
Column R.F.A.

Instructions regarding War Diaries and Intelligence Summaries are contained in F. S. Regs., Part II. and the Staff Manual respectively. Title pages will be prepared in manuscript.

Place	Date	Hour	Summary of Events and Information	Remarks and references to Appendices
	OCTOBER			
LOUVENCOURT	8,9,10		Heavy demands on S.A.A. wagons for R.E. and other service. Heavy ammunition supply.	Zwar
	11	3 pm	C.R.A. inspects lines. Operation Order 5 arrives at 6.45 p.m.	Zwar
	12		1 man, several mules wounded while taking T.M. Bombs up to HÉBUTERNE (T.G.a. central)	Zwar
	13	3 pm	Lt Col C.McL. ROBERTSON rejoins unit from sick leave. Fair ammunition supply from Dump.	Zwar
	14		Normal ammunition supply.	Zwar
	15		R.E. Service cancelled. Ammunition supply normal.	Zwar
	16	6 p.m.	Operation Order No. 55 received. D.A.C. not affected. 78 Remounts for Division arrive in lines at 11 p.m.	Zwar
	17		B. Echelon completes to establishment in gun ammunition. Remounts distributes at 3 p.m. Operation Order No. 56 received 10 p.m. 51/V T.M. Battery joins D.A.C. in afternoon. 1 Officer attaches from 260 Brigade R.F.A.	Zwar
	18	10 am	D.A.C. and 51/V proceeds via VAUCHELLES to THIÈVRES (T.1.a.7.7) to billets	Zwar
	19	10 am	All 18-pr ammunition wagons and 30 S.A. wagons proceeds to be attached to Brigade wagon lines. Dump removed to P.22. central. Adjutant to Hospital.	Zwar
	20, 21		Heavy ammunition supply at Dump.	Zwar
	22		5 Officers from Base Depôt attaches to D.A.C. pending disposal. Heavy ammunition supply.	Zwar
	23	6.30 pm	Operation Order No. 58 received. Continued heavy ammunition supply.	Zwar
	24		Ammunition supply still very heavy.	Zwar

Army Form C. 2118.

WAR DIARY
of
INTELLIGENCE SUMMARY.
(Erase heading not required.)

Instructions regarding War Diaries and Intelligence Summaries are contained in F. S. Regs., Part II. and the Staff Manual respectively. Title pages will be prepared in manuscript.

Place	Date	Hour	Summary of Events and Information	Remarks and references to Appendices
THIEVRES	OCTOBER			
	25	11 am.	18 pr. ammunition wagons returned from Brigades. Further 20 G.S. wagons sent from D.A.C. for attachment to Brigades	E.W.A.
	26		Section 1 moved to new field at FAMÉCHON (C.26.d.5.0). Moderate amm. supply from Dump.	E.W.A.
	27		Heavy ammunition supply. Large allotment of gun ammunition (18 pr.) dumped at H.Q. D.A.C. at midnight.	E.W.A.
	28		Sections completed & establishment from Dump at H.Q. D.A.C. Surplus sent to Dump.	E.W.A.
	29		Section 2 moved to new field at FAMÉCHON. 1 officer (of 5 reinforcements) attached T.M. School.	E.W.A.
	30		1 officer (of the 5 reinforcements) posted to 256 Brigade R.F.A. Heavy ammunition supply. Adjutant	E.W.A.
	31		Heavy ammunition supply.	returned to duty from Hospital) E.W.A.
			Weather during month cold with much rain. Roads very heavy and wagon lines very muddy.	E.W.A.

J. N. Alexander Capt & Adj
for Lieut Colonel Comndg 51 D.A.C.

Vol 15

War Diary
of
51st (Highland) Divisional Ammunition Column R.F.A.
for
November 1916.

Army Form C. 2118.

WAR DIARY
or
INTELLIGENCE SUMMARY.
(Erase heading not required.)

51st D.A.C.

Place	Date	Hour	Summary of Events and Information	Remarks and references to Appendices
THIEVRES	1916 Nov 1		Headquarters established at I.1.d.77. Ammunition Dump established at FOREVILLE (P.22 central Sheet 57.D).	2 war.
	2, 3		Heavy ammunition supply from Dump.	2 war.
	4.		250 men, 500 animals from Brigades attached DAC for rest. Heavy ammunition supply from Dump.	2 war.
	5.		14 remounts arrives for DAC.	2 war.
	6	11 am	Remounts distributed among Sections.	2 war.
	7		Lt. WILSON (260 Bde. a.v. DAC.) left to take up appointment as Adjutant Fifth Army T.M. School. Heavy ammunition supply from Dump.	2 war.
	8,9,10,11		Weather bad. Lines still in bad condition. Heavy ammunition supply from Dump.	2 war.
	12.	10 am	Headquarters removed to FAMECHON (C.20.B)	2 war.
	13,14,15.		Heavy ammunition supply from Dump. Captain J.R. COOPER rejoines unit from ENGLAND on 13th.	2 war.
	16		Medium T.M. Batteries arrives and attaches to DAC.	2 war.
	17,18,19 20,21,22		Heavy ammunition supply. Roads hardening.	2 war.
	23	6 A.m.	Operation Order No. 61 received.	2 war.
	24		after handing over to 37th Division, Personnel at Dump rejoines DAC. Operation Order No. 62 received. 11 am. Preparations made for move.	2 war.
	25	4.30 am	Proceeds via AUTHIE, BUS, BERTRANCOURT, BEAUSSART, MAILLY-MAILLET, HEDAUVILLE and BOUZINCOURT to	2 war.

Army Form C. 2118.

WAR DIARY
INTELLIGENCE SUMMARY.
(Erase heading not required.)

Place	Date	Hour	Summary of Events and Information	Remarks and references to Appendices
FIELD	1916 Nov. 25.		Fields at W.20.d. Arrives 12.30 p.m. in torrential rain. 1 Marquee, 8 bell tents, 100 trench covers allotted to D.A.C. from Camp Commandants store.	War.
	26.		Ground in extremely wet & muddy condition. Large kit parade.	War.
	27.		4 ammunition dumps taken over from 18th, 19th Canadian Divisions. 12 wagons teams attached Fields. R.E. for duty. C.R.A. & Staff Captain visited lines in afternoon. Echelon of C/260 Bty. R.F.A. joined D.A.C. and attached to Echelons 3 & 4, "A" echelon going to section 3, & "B" echelon to Section 4.	War.
	28.		Ground muddy & transport very difficult.	War.
	29.		2 Rdrs, 100 L.D. 2 H.D. remounts arrived from VARENNES for Divisional Artillery. Weather improving. Hard frost at night.	War.
	30.	10 a.m.	Remounts distributed D.A.C. allotted 15 L.D. 50 sets tent bottoms arrives in evening for Div. Arty. 24 wagons (G.S.) attached Batteries.	War.
			Weather during this month was very trying — for the most part cold and wet. Roads & fields in bad state — transport very difficult and great deal of sickness among the men towards end of month, but conditions now improved. Animals standing it well in spite of wet & mud although no cover or standings available. *Gun ammunition dumps at: W.24.n.F.9.2 W.16.c.2.0 and E.H.C.8.6 {ALBERT COMBINED SHEET.} Grenade dumps at:—	War. War.

J. W. Auxerooth Capt. RDA

Vol 16

War Diary
of
51st (Highland) Divisional Ammunition Column R.F.A
for
December, 1916.

WAR DIARY

INTELLIGENCE SUMMARY

51st (Highland) Divisional Ammunition Column R.F.A.

Army Form C. 2118.

Places	Date	Hour	Summary of Events and Information	Remarks and references to Appendices
BRICKFIELDS ARA. (W. 16. b. Cent S.W.)	Dec 1916. 1.	10 a.m.	2 officers 50 or reinforcements arrived from Base and attached D.A.C. Pending disposal in Divisional Artillery. Heavy demands on wagons for R.E. services.	S.11.12.
	2		Site of new Amn. Dump fixed on AVELUY — LA BOISELLE Road at W.18.a.8.7 (Combined Shoot). Preparations commenced for erection of platforms, traverses, for ammunition.	S.11.12.
	3		2 officers 50 or rates to Brigades. All available T.M. personnel attacked D.A.C. detailed for work at gun position of F.A. Boles.	S.W.12.
	4, 5, 6		Continuation of preparation of new dump. Heavy demands for transport of R.E. material	2.W.12.
	7		37 or reinforcements, attached D.A.C. Pending disposal in Divisional Artillery	2.W.12.
	8		Heavy ammunition demands. Lt. Col. C.McL. Robertson admitted to Hospital.	7.W.12.
	9		Heavy ammunition demands. + R.E. services.	2.W.12.
	10		Demands for ammunition still heavy. Horse lines in very muddy condition on account of continuous heavy rain. Ammunition Dump at W.18.a.8.7 now in order and issues made from there.	2.W.12.
	11, 12, 13, 14, 15, 16, 17		Gun ammunition supply. Heavy wagon fatigues. Several wagons sent to I.O.M. for repair.	S.W.12.
	18		One of the sheds of the Divisional Grenade Dump at W.16.C.1.0. caught fire about 10 p.m. Cause unknown. Fire blazed till about midnight & a considerable quantity of rockets flares lost. Sheds completely destroyed.	2.W.12.
	19		Usual heavy R.E. services.	2.W.12.

WAR DIARY
INTELLIGENCE SUMMARY

Army Form C. 2118.

Instructions regarding War Diaries and Intelligence Summaries are contained in F. S. Regs., Part II. and the Staff Manual respectively. Title pages will be prepared in manuscript.

(Erase heading not required.)

Place	Date	Hour	Summary of Events and Information	Remarks and references to Appendices
BRICKFIELDS AREA	DEC R. 20	10 am	Court of Enquiry sat at HQ DAC to enquire into and report on the cause of the fire which occurred at Sir Granada Drunk	Inter
		1 pm	Inspection of lines by C.R.A. & Staff Captain	Inter
	21, 22		Heavy R.E. services, owing every available to wagon to be out.	Inter
	23		Lt. Col. C. McL. Robertson returned from hospital.	Inter
	24, 25	10.30 am	Usual heavy R.E. services. Heavy ammunition supply. Captain J.A. Thomson, 2nd Res Cavalry Regt attached DAC as Veterinary Officer to Div. Arty.	Inter
	26	3 pm	C.R.A. inspects DAC in afternoon. Pt of reinforcements arrived from Base and attached DAC pending disposal in Div. Arty.	Inter
	27, 28		Fair ammunition supply. Usual R.E. duties.	Inter
	29		34 or. reinforcements posted to Udeo.	Inter
	30, 31		Usual heavy R.E. services. Fair ammunition supply.	Inter
			Weather during month, wet roads. Lines & roads in very muddy condition.	

Winterson ft Col.
51st D. A. C.

Vol 17

CONFIDENTIAL
No 71 (1)
HIGHLAND
DIVISION.

War Diary

of

51st (Highland) Divisional Ammunition Column R.F.A.

For

January 1917.

CONFIDENTIAL

No 21(i)

WAR DIARY
of
HIGHLAND DIVISION
INTELLIGENCE SUMMARY.
(Erase heading not required.)

Army Form C. 2118.

51st (Highland) Division Jan1 to Jan6. pm

Instructions regarding War Diaries and Intelligence Summaries are contained in F. S. Regs., Part II. and the Staff Manual respectively. Title pages will be prepared in manuscript.

Place	Date 1917	Hour	Summary of Events and Information	Remarks and references to Appendices
FIELD	JANUARY 1		Hdd. encamped in BOUZINCOURT - ALBERT ROAD (W.2.d. sheet 57D). Arrangements being made to fill up to establishment in Guns Ammn. pending move.	Invar
	2.		Preparations for early move.	Invar
	3rd		Heavy mgm fatigue. Continuation of preparations for move.	Invar
			Orders received to move S.A.A. & other wagons via FIÉNVILLERS till completion of move. Orders for R.E. to remain with Divn.	Invar
	5.		Orders received 4 pm. 33 orr reinforcements posted to Brigades. Remainder posted to Dac.	Invar
	6.	10am	Divn. left BRICKFIELDS area. Proceeded via BOUZINCOURT, ACHEUX, LOUVENCOURT to SARTON area. (F.S.2.H. Lens 11) Operation order iss. 8pm	Invar
	7.	9.30 am	Divn. left SARTON area. Proceeded via DOULLENS & MEZEROLLES & OUTREBOIS (C.H.23 Lens 11). Operation order received 8.30 pm.	Invar
	8.	9 am	Divn. left MEZEROLLES area. Proceeded via AUXI-LE-CHATEAU to FROYELLES (L.H. 2.8. ABBEVILLE)	Invar
	9.	1 am	Operation order received. Divn. left FROYELLES at 10am and proceeded via LE PLESSIER & DRUCAT to CAOURS & G.O. LAVIERS (H.Q. 1 & 2 at CAOURS).	Invar
	10.		5 officers, reinforcements, at Divn. finding disposal in divisions.	Invar
	11.		12 Orr. reinforcements, posted to Divn.	Invar
	12.	10 pm	Operation order received.	Invar
	13.	10.30am	Divn. proceeded via L'HEURE, ABBEVILLE, LAVIERS, PORT-LE-GRAND to NOYELLES-SUR-MER (I.4.5.2. ABBEVILLE). 5 officers, reinforcements, posted to Brigades.	Invar
	14.		Supervision of billets commenced.	Invar
	15.		C.R.A. visits Divn. in afternoon. Preparation of scheme of Recreational Training in Division. Naval fatigue. Cleaning & improving billets. Overhaul of wagons & equipment. Drill classes. Riding School &c. commenced continues till end of month.	Invar
	16-21.			
	18.		3 wagons despatched to RUE to hay for Division.	Invar
	19.		Visit from C.R.A. 18 Orr. reinforcements att. D.A.C. finding disposal.	Invar
	20.		22 Orr. reinforcements att. Divn. finding disposal.	Invar
	22.76.		Reorganisation of Divn. commenced nearly No. 3 Section taken up to complete "A" Echelon to new establishment. Sub lists of surplus personnel, animals, wagons &c. made.	Invar
	22.		30 Orr. reinforcements att. Divn. finding disposal.	Invar
	23.		2 wagons to RUE to hay for Division. Divn. took over Sma grenade dump at BUIGNY-ST-MACLOU (J.5.8.9).	Invar
	76.		Orders received to hand over to 3rd Division 10 limbers 60 wagons to 10 sma carts. Only 9 limb. 60 wagons were handed over, as only 9 sma carts were received from 3rd Division.	Invar

Army Form C. 2118.

WAR DIARY
INTELLIGENCE SUMMARY.

51st (Highland) Divisional Ammunition Column

(Erase heading not required.)

Instructions regarding War Diaries and Intelligence Summaries are contained in F. S. Regs., Part II. and the Staff Manual respectively. Title pages will be prepared in manuscript.

Place	Date	Hour	Summary of Events and Information	Remarks and references to Appendices
field	1917 Jan 26		Reorganization completed in respect of tractors 12 mt. surplus personnel, animals, vehicles embodied in details of No. 3 Section pending disposal.	
	27		4 officers, reinforcements, awaited Dvr. finding disposal in division.	
	28		Naval Brigade 4 officers posted to F.A. Bdes.	
	29		Brigades drew from details No. 3 Section to make up their deficiencies in animals. 76 or. reinforcements posted to Brigades, remainder to Dpt.	
	30		Grenade dump removed from BUIGNY-ST. MACLOU to NOYELLES, wagons arriving NOYELLES at 4 p.m. fair amounts of S.A. Amm. by Lght. Brigades.	
	31		Grenades, rockets &c. from dump at MILLENCOURT removed to NOYELLES.	
			Weather during week frosty but dry. Roads kept and hard lines in good condition.	

J. W. Alexander
Capt. & Adj.
for Major
Commanding 51 D.A.C.

Vol 18

War Diary of 51st (Highland) Divisional Ammunition Column R.F.A. for February, 1917.

WAR DIARY or INTELLIGENCE SUMMARY

Army Form C. 2118.

51st (Highland) Divisional Ammunition Column R.F.A.

Instructions regarding War Diaries and Intelligence Summaries are contained in F.S. Regs., Part II. and the Staff Manual respectively. Title pages will be prepared in manuscript.

(Erase heading not required.)

Place	Date 1917	Hour	Summary of Events and Information	Remarks and references to Appendices
NOVELLES-S-MER	FEBY 1		Reorganization of D.A.C. completed and surplus personnel ready to be transferred. Annual Fatigues.	2W12
	2	1000 hors	S.A.A. received from 51st A.S.P. on account of Establishment. Orders received to send 61 o.r. & riders, 118 L.D.& G.S. wagons and 16 ammunition wagons surplus to establishment to join 63rd (R.N.) Divn Arty.	2W12
	3	10 a.m.	61 o.r. with animals and vehicles as detailed, proceeded to join 63rd (R.N.) Divn Arty. Operation Order No. 109 received. 5.30 pm. Preparations for move.	2W12
	4	11 a.m.	Remainder of surplus vehicles — 3 GS wagons and 8 ammunition wagons — sent to Ordnance Dept ABBÉVILLE.	2W12
	5	9.45 am to 7 pm	D.A.C. left NOVELLES-SUR-MER and proceeded via SAILLY-LE-SEC - LE TITRE - to GUESCHART (LENS II - A.11.9) arriving here at 4 p.m. Operation Order No. 70 received.	2W12
	6	9.15 am	D.A.C. left GUESCHART and proceeded via OUEUX - FILLIEVRES to AUBROMETZ & BOUBERS. HQ + "A" Echelon at AUBROMETZ, "B" Echelon to BOUBERS. Progress difficult owing to slippery state of roads, due to severe frost. Operation Order No. 71 received at 9 pm.	2W12
	7	7.20 am	D.A.C. left AUBROMETZ and BOUBERS and proceeded to BEAUVOIS (C.2.8.7) arriving at 2 p.m. Operation Order 72 received at 6 p.m.	2W12
	8	9.45 am	D.A.C. left BEAUVOIS and proceeded via ST POL to LA COMTÉ (F.I.Q.I.) arriving at 4 p.m.	2W12
	9		22 G.S. wagons attached to Infantry Brigade to assist them in moving.	2W12
	10	5 pm.	Operation Order received. "B" Echelon to proceed to FREVIN CAPELLE. Heavy demands on ammunition for R.E. Service.	2W12
	11	11 am.	"B" Echelon proceeded to FREVIN CAPELLE. Divisional Reserve Magazine at MAROEUIL taken over by D.A.C. 1 officer & 20 in charge. 45 o.r. sent to brigades. 100 o.r. sent as working parties to dig T.M. Positions, Billets in ARRAS.	2W12
	12			2W12
	13		S/Sgt CMSL ROBERTSON reported from I month's leave. 5 GS wagons complete attached to R. Railway Co. R.E. MAROEUIL.	2W12
	14		NCO & 9 o.r.s attached to duty at ammunition dump near FREVIN CAPELLE. 10 GS wagons to duty with 18th Echelon Regt. ACA for road repair. 10 GS wagons to 306th. Road Construction Co ACA for road repair wagons reporting daily. Brigades for this duty. 3 GS wagons attached to 401st (Highland) Field Co RE. 3 GS wagons attached to 4th (Highland) Field Co RE.	2W12
	15-16		Horse Fatigues and carting out of harness wagon equipment.	2W12
	17		26 o.r. reinforcements attached D.A.C.	2W12
	18		Operation Order No. 73 received. 23 o.r. posted as reinforcements to Brigades. 3 returned to D.A.C.	2W12
	19		Heavy demands on G.S. wagons for Fatigues.	2W12
	20		Preparations for move.	2W12
	21	9.30 am	"A" Echelon left LA COMTÉ and proceeded via OURTON, DIVION to CAMBLAIN-CHATELAIN arriving here at 12 noon. Working party of 1 NCO and 5 men attached to RE Dump at MAROEUIL.	2W12
	22		Operation Order received. "A" Echelon to move on 23rd.	2W12
	23	9.30 am	"A" Echelon of D.A.C. left CAMBLAIN-CHATELAIN and proceeded via DIVION to CAUCOURT. HQ proceeded to AGNIÈRES nr AUBIGNY.	2W12

A5834 Wt.W4973 M687 750,000 8/16 D.D.& L. Ltd. Forms/C.2118/13.

Army Form C. 2118.

WAR DIARY
or
INTELLIGENCE SUMMARY.
5ᵗʰ (Highland) Divisional Ammunition Column R.F.A.

(Erase heading not required.)

Instructions regarding War Diaries and Intelligence Summaries are contained in F. S. Regs., Part II. and the Staff Manual respectively. Title pages will be prepared in manuscript.

Place	Date	Hour	Summary of Events and Information	Remarks and references to Appendices
	1917 FEBY			
	23		Billets in AGNIERES very scarce	¾wa
	24		1 Officer, 1 guard detached for duty to Corps Ammunition Dump at AGAIZ. Rest at AGNIERES. "A" Echelon at CROISILLES. "B" Echelon at FREVIN CAPELLE. Normal ammunition supply of gun ammunition. Heavy supply of 2" T.M.	¾wa
	25		Fair ammunition supply.	¾wa
	26		H.Q. of digging party at T.M. Positions rejoined D.A.C. 6 or reinforcements detached from base to D.A.C. Party of 30 on duty for duty under Town Major FREVIN CAPELLE.	¾wa
	27		6 or joined D.A.C. Usual fatigues. Heavy ammunition supply. 1 or posted to 76 Bde R.F.A	¾wa
	28		Usual fatigues. Heavy ammunition supply.	¾wa
			Weather during first part of month very frosty. During later part snowing and wet.	

J. W. Alexander Capᵗ R.A
for Lt. Colonel
Commdg 51ˢᵗ D. A. C

Vol 19

War Diary
Of
51st (Highland) Divisional Ammunition Column R.F.A.
For
March, 1917.

WAR DIARY or INTELLIGENCE SUMMARY

Army Form C. 2118.

(Erase heading not required.)

Instructions regarding War Diaries and Intelligence Summaries are contained in F. S. Regs., Part II. and the Staff Manual respectively. Title pages will be prepared in manuscript.

Place	Date 1917	Hour	Summary of Events and Information	Remarks and references to Appendices
FIELD			REFERENCE SHEETS LENS 11 & 51c.	
	March 1		Headquarters D.A.C. 262 at AGNIÈRES (E.B.C. 12, 51c) "A" Echelon at CAUCOURT (G.B.8.8 LENS 11) "B" Echelon at FREVIN CAPELLE (E. 10.c central 51c) Ammunition Dumps at ACQ no.1 and 2 (E.11.d 49 51c) under charge of DAC officer. Divisional Grenade Magazine at MAROEUIL (F 27 d. 51c). Fair ammunition supply from Dumps.	—
	2-3		Heavy ammunition supply from Dumps	—
	4.		C.R.A. inspects Headquarters and "B" Echelon, commencing ink Headquarters at 11am. Heavy guns and T.M. amn. supply	—
	5,6,7,8,9		Ammunition supply still extremely heavy. Transport difficult owing to soft nature of ground consequent on heavy rains.	—
	10.		Heavy ammunition supply. 3 officers arrives from Base Depôt and posted to Brigades, 2 to 256 Brigade and 1 to 256 Brigade R.F.A. 16 o.r. attached D.A.C. as reinforcements from Base Depôt.	—
	11		Heavy ammunition supply. 16 o.r. reinforcements posted to Brigade & DAC.	—
	12-13		Continued heavy ammunition supply.	—
	14.	9 am	A Echelon moves from CAUCOURT to FREVIN CAPELLE via AGNIÈRES	—
	15-16		Heavy ammunition supply	—
	17.	3pm	Headquarters DAC moves from AGNIÈRES to FREVIN CAPELLE. Heavy gun & T.M. ammunition supply. Several animals killed and wounded near T.M. Dump, ROCLINCOURT. One man wounded.	—
	18.		57 o.r. reinforcements attached from Base Depôt. Heavy ammunition supply.	—
	19		Abnormal ammunition supply	—
	20.		37 o.r. reinforcements which arrives on 18th posted to Brigades & DAC, 21 to DAC & 16 to Brigades.	—
	21.	12 noon	No 1 Section, DAC moves from FREVIN CAPELLE to MAROEUIL & took over ammunition supply from O.R.D. to gun positions. Light railway.	—
	22		Heavy ammunition supply	—
	23		Heavy ammunition supply	—
	24, 25		Abnormal ammunition supply	—
	26		Heavy ammunition supply. 1 o.r. wounded by M.G. fire at T.M. dump, ROCLINCOURT while delivering T.M. ammunition. New Ammunition Dump established at ACQ (E.11.a central 51c) under charge of a DAC officer. Heavy ammunition supply.	—
	27		Heavy ammunition supply. 80 o.r. reinforcements attached from Base Depôt.	—
	28		Heavy ammunition supply. 80 o.r. reinforcements posted to Brigade & DAC. - 4 to 255 Bde RFA, 16 to DAC. Heavy ammunition supply. Dumps kept very busy owing to the agreement of 34, 84 & 315 Army F.A. Bdes to the Divisional Artillery	—
	30, 31		Abnormal ammunition supply	—
			Weather during month wet and roads & lines in muddy condition. Transport difficult	—

Vol 20

War Diary
of
51st (Highland) Divisional Ammunition Column, R.F.A.
for
April, 1917.

51st D.A.C.

Army Form C. 2118.

WAR DIARY
INTELLIGENCE SUMMARY
(Erase heading not required.)

Instructions regarding War Diaries and Intelligence Summaries are contained in F.S. Regs., Part II. and the Staff Manual respectively. Title pages will be prepared in manuscript.

Place	Date	Hour	Summary of Events and Information	Remarks and references to Appendices
Field	1917. April.		Reference Sheets 51 B & 51 C (1/40000)	
	1.		D.A.C. Headquarters established at FREVIN CAPELLE (E.10 central) also No.2 Section & B'Echelon. No.1 Section at MAROEUIL (L.3.a.1t). Heavy ammunition supply to gun positions. 1 O.R. mortally wounded by enemy shrapnel, in MAROEUIL.	zwa
	2.		Ammunition supply very heavy, every available wagon being utilized to keep the Army F.A. Bdes. attached, as well as to supply the 51st Division Brigades. Roads very heavy owing to continuous snow and rain.	zwa
	3-4-5.		Ammunition supply still abnormal. Roads still heavy.	zwa
	6.		Very heavy ammunition supply. 1 O.R. mortally wounded while delivering T.M. ammunition at ROCLINCOURT 51B. (A.29.c) No.1 Section billets in MAROEUIL in evening. 2 O.R. slightly wounded	zwa
	7-8		Ammunition supply still abnormal. Roads drying up.	zwa
	9	5.30 am	VIMY RIDGE attack begun. D.A.C. standing by ready to move forward.	zwa
	10.	6 pm	D.A.C. moved to new area at ANZIN (C.1.b.d.) 51B HQ established in MAROEUIL (L.3.a.9.9.) 5 officers 20 O.R. reinforcements arrived at FREVIN CAPELLE for Div Arty. & billeted in FREVIN CAPELLE for the night. Night stormy, with heavy snow showers	zwa
	11.		Improving of horse standings at ANZIN. Heavy rains.	zwa
	12.		5 officers 30 O.R. posted to Bdes. 5 O.R. to D.A.C.	zwa
	13.		Heavy ammunition supply.	zwa
	14.		18 O.R. reinforcements attached D.A.C. Heavy ammunition supply. 18 O.R. posted to Bdes. & D.A.C.	zwa

WAR DIARY
INTELLIGENCE SUMMARY.
(Erase heading not required.)

Army Form C. 2118.

51 D.A.C.   2.

Place	Date	Hour	Summary of Events and Information	Remarks and references to Appendices
Field	1917 April 15-16-17		Heavy ammunition supply. Grounds drying up.	2WDA
	18		Sections 1,2 "B" Echelon moved to new area at G.17.c.7.6 (51D). Very heavy ammunition supply. Roads heavy & transport difficult.	2WDA
	19		Heavy ammunition supply.	2WDA
	20		Sections 1,2 "D" Echelon moved back to wagon lines at ANZIN. Ammunition supply very heavy, very wagon being utilized. 1 officer 29 o.r. reinforcements reached D.A.C., pending disposal.	2WDA
	21-22		Heavy ammunition supply. Roads & fields drying up.	2WDA
	23		Heavy ammunition supply. D.A.C. standing to, prepared for further advance. 1 off. posted to D.A.C. 29 o.r. to Base.	2WDA
	24		Abnormal ammunition supply. Orders coming in all night. Wagon lines shelled by enemy guns. Fora killed. Instructions received to bring in from forward area, 3 captured German field guns duty received throughout to T.H.Q.	2WDA
	25-30		Heavy ammunition supply. Roads in good condition transport easier. A very strenuous month. Weather for first 3 weeks very bad — heavy rains with snow showers. Last week fine, and conditions greatly improved.	2WDA

T. N. Anderson Capt. Dcy.
Commdg. 51' D.A.C.

Vol 21

War Diary
of
51st (Highland) Divisional Ammunition Column R.F.A.
for
May. 1917

Army Form C. 2118.

WAR DIARY
INTELLIGENCE SUMMARY.
51st (Highland) Divisional Ammn. Col. R.F.A.

(Erase heading not required.)

Instructions regarding War Diaries and Intelligence Summaries are contained in F.S. Regs., Part II. and the Staff Manual respectively. Title pages will be prepared in manuscript.

Place	Date	Hour	Summary of Events and Information	Remarks and references to Appendices
FIELD	MAY 1917.			
	1		D.A.C. Headquarters at MAROEUIL (L.3.a.51.c). Sections at G.1.7.d (51.B).	Ammn.
			NICOLAS & Advanced Divisional Brenade Magazine at H.13.c. (51.B). Both under charge of D.A.C. officer.	
			No II Anzin Dump, MADAGASCAR Dump and XVII Corps "F" Dump all under charge of D.A.C. officers. Heavy ammunition supply.	
	2		Heavy ammunition supply to gun positions.	Ammn.
	3		Abnormal ammunition supply. 27 O.R. attached from R.H. R.F.A. Base Depôt to D.A.C. pending disposal.	Ammn.
	4		Heavy ammunition supply.	Ammn.
	5		Heavy ammunition supply. 27 O.R. reinforcements posted to Brigades & D.A.C.	Ammn.
	6–11		Continue heavy supply of ammunition to battery positions. Roads bars & dry, & transport easy.	Ammn.
	12		Abnormal ammunition supply. 75 O.R. reinforcements attached to D.A.C. from R.H. R.F.A. Base Depôt.	Ammn.
	13		Heavy ammunition supply.	Ammn.
	14		Heavy ammunition supply. 75 O.R. posted to Brigades & D.A.C.	Ammn.
	15, 16		Heavy ammunition supply.	Ammn.
	17		XVII Corps "F" (Forward) gun dump closed down and D.A.C. officer i/c rejoins unit.	Ammn.
	18		Abnormal ammunition supply.	Ammn.

A McMain Lieut.
a/Adjt. for O.C. 51 D.A.C.

Army Form C. 2118.

WAR DIARY
INTELLIGENCE SUMMARY. — 51st (Highland) Div Ammunit Rsn
(Erase heading not required.)

Instructions regarding War Diaries and Intelligence Summaries are contained in F. S. Regs., Part II. and the Staff Manual respectively. Title pages will be prepared in manuscript.

Place	Date	Hour	Summary of Events and Information	Remarks and references to Appendices
FIELD	MAY 1917 19	4 a.m.	2 captured German field guns brought in by D.A.C. party i/c Lieut Col C. McL. Robertson from area round FAMPOUX (H.7.51.B), and left in "B" Echelon lines.	Allmen.
	20	3 a.m.	3 captured German field guns brought in by D.A.C. party from FAMPOUX area.	Allmen.
	21, 22		Heavy ammunition supply. Rly wagon teams engaged in transporting ammunition from O/s to new gun positions and removing supplies from old positions. (Battery positions having been moved forward)	Allmen.
	23, 24		Heavy ammunition supply and wagon fatigues at positions & bombs dropped on Echelons on 23rd 30 damp	Allmen.
	25		3 Officers reinforcements, posted from Base depot to D.A.C.	Allmen.
	26-28		Heavy ammunition supply and fatigues at gun positions.	Allmen.
	29		1 Officer reinforcement attached D.A.C. from Base Depot.	Allmen.
	30		Officer reinforcement, posted to 2/51 T.M. Bty. Lieut Col C. McL. Robertson granted 10 days leave.	Allmen.
	31		Heavy ammunition supply. Divisional Reserve Magazine and Advanced Divisional Parade Dump handed over to 9th Division, and turnover resumed D.A.C.	Allmen.
			Weather during month very dry and warm. Ammunition supply heavy during whole month, but dry hard roads made transport easy.	Allmen.

J. McMain Lieut.
a/Adj. for O.C. 51 D.A.C.

No 21(A)
HIGHLAND
DIVISION.

Vol 22

War Diary

of

51st (Highland) Divisional Ammunition Column

For

June 1917

WAR DIARY
or
INTELLIGENCE SUMMARY

(Erase heading not required.)

Army Form C. 2118.

51st (Highland) Divl: Ammunt: Coln:

Place	Date 1917	Hour	Summary of Events and Information	Remarks and references to Appendices
FIELD	June. 1		D.A.C. wagon lines at ANZIN (G.I.6.d.5.51°). Headquarters at MARŒUIL (L.3.a.5.1°). Heavy ammunition supply.	
	2		Heavy ammunition supply. 55 cm reinforcement from R.H.+R.F.A. Base Depot attached D.A.C. pending disposal.	
	3		55 cm reinforcement posted to Brigades and D.A.C. — 9 drivers to D.A.C.	
	4		82 cm reinforcement from R.H.+R.F.A. Base Depot posted to Brigades + D.A.C. — 27 to D.A.C.	
	5		Heavy ammunition supply. Several bombs dropped on billeting lines at ANZIN, by Boche aircraft. No damage done.	
	6		Heavy ammunition supply. 2 Officers reported as reinforcements from R.H.+R.F.A. Base Depot. 1 posted to 255th Brigade R.F.A. and one to D.A.C.	
	7		RFA. and one to D.A.C. Loading: one and 16 drivers from D.A.C. proceeded to No 2 Advanced Remount Depot ABBEVILLE, along with parties of 2 n.c.o. and 256 Brigade R.F.A., to collect 200 L.D. remount for 51st Divisional Artillery.	
	8		26 cm reinforcement attached from R.H. +R.F.A. Base Depot pending disposal. MADAGASCAR CORNER Ammunition Dump handed over to 9th Divisional Artillery at 10 am.	
	9		Heavy ammunition supply.	
	10	1 A.M.	200 L.D. remount arrives from ABBEVILLE and marcheb to Brigade and D.A.C. D.A.C. allocates 36 L.D. Heavy fatigue at Gun Positions, removing empty cartridge cases. Fair ammunition supply.	
	11		Moderate ammunition supply.	
	12		3 mules killed, 1 wounded while taking up ammunition to gun positions.	
	13		51st Divisional Artillery Operation Order No. 82 received. Preparation commences to move.	
	14, 15, 16		Continuation of preparation for move. Moderate ammunition supply.	
	17, 18	9 am	D.A.C. left ANZIN area and proceeded via BRAY, ECOIVRES + ACQ to FREVIN CAPELLE, arriving at noon.	
	19, 20		Bivouacs at FREVIN CAPELLE. Fitting out and cleaning of harness, wagons + equipment.	
	21		2 Officers, 10 OR reinforcement attached D.A.C. from R.H.+R.F.A. Base Depot, pending disposal.	
	22		2 Officers + 19 OR reinforcement posted to Brigades + D.A.C. 2 Officers to 255 Bde. R.F.A. 8 OR. to D.A.C.	
	23		Cleaning + oiling of wagons, harness + equipment in preparation for coming trek.	
	24		C.R.A. visits D.A.C. in forenoon. Continues preparations for move to new area.	
	25, 26, 27 28, 29		Continues preparation for move to new area.	
	30		4 motor lorries allotted to D.A.C. to assist in trek.	

Weather during first half of month very dry and hot, during second half showery. Roads hard and in good condition.

(Sd) _____ Lt Col
    Comdt D.A.C.

CONFIDENTIAL
No. 71(A)
HIGHLAND DIVISION.

23

War Diary

of

51st (Highland) Divisional Ammunition Column. R.F.A.

for

July. 1917.

WAR DIARY

INTELLIGENCE SUMMARY

(Erase heading not required.)

Army Form C. 2118.

51st (Highland) Divisional Ammunition Column R.F.A.

Instructions regarding War Diaries and Intelligence Summaries are contained in F. S. Regs., Part II. and the Staff Manual respectively. Title pages will be prepared in manuscript.

Place	Date	Hour	Summary of Events and Information	Remarks and references to Appendices
FIELD.	1917 JULY 1	4 am	D.A.C. left FREVIN CAPELLE (P.D.C.) and proceeded via SAVY-BERLETTE, VANDELICOURT & TINCQUES to ROELLECOURT and RAMECOURT (St. POL area), arriving here about 9.20 am.	Pivotin
	2	3 pm	Operation Order No. 85 received from HQ Divisional Artillery, and preparations commenced for move on following day.	Pivotin
	3	4 am	D.A.C. left ROELLECOURT and RAMECOURT and proceeded via PERNES, FLORINGHEM and FERFAY to AMETTES and NEDON (Square E 6, HAZEBROUCK 5A Sheet), arriving at 9 am. after long hot march. Operation Order no. 86 received at 3 pm.	Pivotin
	4	6 am	D.A.C. left AMETTES and NEDON and proceeded via AMES, St. HILAIRE and MAZINGHEM to AIRE and NEUFPRÉ (Square E5, HAZEBROUCK 5A SHEET), arriving at 9.30 am in heavy rain. Operation Order No. 87 received at 3 pm.	Pivotin
	5	5.30 am	DR left AIRE and NEUFPRÉ and proceeded via PECQUEUR, LA BELLE HOTESSE and WALLON CAPPEL to STAPLE area (Square U9 Red 27), arriving about 9 am. Operation Order No. 88 received at 3 pm.	Pivotin
	6	5.30 am	D.A.C. left STAPLE area and proceeded via QUEVE D'OXELAERE, OXELAERE and STEENVOORDE to GODEWAERSVELDE area (Squares 11 and 18. Red 27), arriving at 10 am. Operation Order No. 89 received at 2 pm. Advance party proceeded to reconnoitre wagon lines & prepare grounds for occupation.	Pivotin
	7	5.30 am	D.A.C. left GODEWAERSVELDE area and proceeded via STEENVOORDE — POPERINGHE Road through POPERINGHE to wagon lines in PESELHOEK area (A. 27 a. Red 28), arriving at 10 am. Enemy shelling area pretty heavily with H.E. Horse lines situated in long wooded avenue of trees. Enemy aircraft active over area at night, dropping bombs. No damage done to D.A.C. lines.	Pivotin

Army Form C. 2118.

WAR DIARY
or
INTELLIGENCE SUMMARY.
(Erase heading not required.) 51st (Highland) Divisional Ammunition Column R.F.A.

Instructions regarding War Diaries and Intelligence Summaries are contained in F. S. Regs., Part II. and the Staff Manual respectively. Title pages will be prepared in manuscript.

Place	Date	Hour	Summary of Events and Information	Remarks and references to Appendices
FIELD	1917 July 8		Very heavy rain in early morning turned roads and fields into morass. 50 O.R. attached to D.T.M.O. 11th Division, for fatigue work in forward area. 3 officers attached 11th D.A.C. to assist that unit in ammunition supply. 1 O.R & 2 officers posted to 51st T.M. Batteries. I.T.M. officer posted to D.A.C. Enemy shelling area south of lines at frequent intervals.	Fwia.
	9		Belgian interpreter attached from Belgian Mission to D.A.C. Heavy wagon fatigues on R.E. duties.	Fwia.
	10		1 O.R. of fatigue party attached D.T.M.O. killed in action.	Fwia.
	11	10 a.m.	Ammunition dumps at TROIS TOURS and BURNT FARM taken over by D.A.C. 3 officers rejoined from 11th D.A.C. Enemy continuously shelling area. Enemy aircraft active at night, dropping bombs. Heavy ammunition supply to dump at TROIS TOURS.	Fwia.
	12		1 O.R. reinforcement posted to D.A.C. from Base depôt. 3 O.R. and several animals wounded while delivering amm. to TROIS TOURS dump.	Fwia.
	13		Heavy ammunition supply. Pack animals used to transport ammunition from TROIS TOURS dump, across the Canal to BURNT FARM (C.20.c Sheet 28). 1 O.R. mortally wounded, and several animals killed and wounded, at this duty.	Fwia.
	14		Continued "packing" of ammunition across canal to BURNT FARM. Several animals wounded. 3 officers, reinforcements reported from Base depôt, and posted to 258th Brigade R.F.A. Advanced Divisional S.A.A. and Grenade Dump EAST of POND Cottage, at C.19.d (Sheet 28) taken over by D.A.C. and 6 O.R. detailed to duty here.	Fwia.
	15		3 O.R. of forward fatigue party wounded (1 mortally) by enemy shell fire. Several pack animals killed & wounded	Fwia.

2353 Wt. W.2544/1454 700,000 5/15 D. D. & L. A.D.S.S./Forms/C. 2118.

WAR DIARY

INTELLIGENCE SUMMARY.

(Erase heading not required) 51st (Highland) Divisional Ammunition Column, R.F.A.

Army Form C. 2118.

Place	Date	Hour	Summary of Events and Information	Remarks and references to Appendices
FIELD	1917 JULY 16		Heavy ammunition supply to Battery positions	Ewra
	17		Heavy supply of 4.5" ammunition (fuze 106) to Battery positions. Fatigue party from D.A.C. under 1 officer employed daily in fixing fuze 106 into 4.5" ammunition at "DIRTY BUCKET" Refilling Point. 15 wagon loads of 20 pounds taken from D.A.C. lines to IRISH FARM under an officer of Special Co., R.E., coming under heavy shell fire.	Ewra
	18		Continued heavy supply of 4.5" amm. (fuze 106). 3 G.S. wagon loads of Gas ammo to IRISH FARM.	Ewra
	19		Heavy ammunition supply and R.E. fatigues. Enemy shelling area with H.E.	Ewra
	20		3 O.R. wounded at TROIS TOURS (DTMO's fatigue party).	Ewra
	21		6 O.R. wounded while taking ammunition up to Batteries. Heavy ammunition supply. Enemy continues to shell area. Fatigue party attached DTMO relieved by fresh party	Ewra
	22		1 Colonel, R.F.A. attached D.A.C. Heavy ammunition supply.	Ewra
	23		Heavy ammunition supply. 3 officers, reinforcements, reported from Base Depôt, and posted, 1 to 256th and 2 to 255th Brigade R.F.A. 1 O.R. attached advanced "Grenade Dump" wounded in action by enemy shell fire.	Ewra
	24		Heavy R.E. fatigue. 2 O.R. wounded and several animals killed and wounded by enemy shell fire in Det. lines about 8 p.m. Supply of ammunition to Gnri Battery (39th division). Refilling party now working at XVIII Corps Ammunition Refilling Point (A.23.a. Sheet 28), owing to "DIRTY BUCKET" Dump having been destroyed by enemy shell fire.	Ewra

WAR DIARY
—of—
INTELLIGENCE SUMMARY.

(Erase heading not required.) 51st (Highland) Divisional Ammunition Column, R.F.A.

Army Form C. 2118.

Place	Date	Hour	Summary of Events and Information	Remarks and references to Appendices
FIELD	1917 JULY 25		Completion of supply of ammunition to B/241 Battery, R.F.A. BURNT FARM Dump hit by enemy shell-fire, and much of the ammunition destroyed. No casualties.	
	26.		Heavy ammunition supply. Advanced Grenade Dump hit by enemy shells, and a quantity of grenade, rockets, etc. destroyed. No casualties.	
	27.		Instructions received to refill BURNT FARM Dump. Pack animals left Dpt. about midnight with ammunition, and new dump formed west of BURNT FARM, this dump being called BURNT FARM WEST Dump, and attacked midway between Canal and BURNT FARM. 2 animals killed, on this duty.	
	28.		Continuation of pack transport of ammunition to BURNT FARM WEST Dump, animals leaving at midnight. Enemy aircraft active over area, dropping bombs in vicinity of Dpt. lines.	
	29.		3 O.R. wounded on pack transport duty. Very heavy rain rendered roads soft and muddy. Enemy shells over leaving in afternoon.	
	30.		Continuation of pack transport of amm. to BURNT FARM WEST Dump. 1 O.R. wounded, while attached to R.T.O. POPERINGHE.	
	31	5.15 a.m.	Dpt. left wagon lines in PESELHOEK area and proceeded via ELVERDINGHE ROAD to new wagon lines near HOSPITAL FARM. - at B 26.a (Sheet 28), arriving at 9 a.m. Fatigue party, attached to D.T.M.O. relieved and rejoined Dpt. 1 officer + 50 o.r. att. Report centre, R.E. for special duty. Heavy amm. supply.	

Vol 24

War Diary
of
51st Highland Divisional Ammn Col
for
August, 1917.

Army Form C. 2118.

WAR DIARY
or
INTELLIGENCE SUMMARY.
(Erase heading not required.)

51st (Highland) Divisional Ammunition Column, R.F.A.

Place	Date 1917	Hour	Summary of Events and Information	Remarks and references to Appendices
Field	August 1		D.A.C. encamped at B.26.a. (Sheet 28) Roads and lines very soft and muddy on account of heavy rains. "KOA" ammunition commences and first consignments of ammunition arrives.	Swa.
	2. 3		Heavy ammunition supply by pack animals to gun positions. Roads very heavy and transport extremely difficult.	Swa. Swa.
	4		Heavy ammunition supply. 26 o.r. reinforcements from R.H. and R.F.A. Base Depot attached pending disposal.	Swa.
	5		Heavy ammunition supply by pack and wagon to gun positions. Enemy aircraft active at night & several bombs dropped in vicinity of camp.	Swa.
	6		Roads and lines hardening up under the influence of sun and wind. Heavy ammunition supply from KOA dump to gun positions.	Swa. Swa.
	7	5.30am	Animals & HQ and No 1 section sent to XVIII Corps Horse dump to be supplied Heavy ammunition supplies rejoined D.A.C. Heavy ammunition supply by pack and wagon. Arrival of 20 officers and parties in charge aur of divisional Grenade Dump transferred over to 11th division and parties in charge and to Horsdorph.	Swa.
	8			Swa.
	9		New Ammunition Refilling Point for Left Group, formed at VLAMERTINGHE - BRIELEN Road at H.H. & 05.95 (Sheet 28) and party of 2 officers and 6 o.r. from D.A.C. sent in charge of it. 1 officer. 50 o.r. from labor corps sent as working party. This Refilling Point to be known as "B" Refilling Point. 19 o.r. reinforcements from R.H. + R.F.A. Base Depot attached pending disposal. 26 o.r. bombs to Brigades. Abnormal ammunition supply. KOA being run out.	Swa.
	10.		Abnormal ammunition supply.	Swa.
	11.		KOA dump run out, and all ammunition to Left Group being supplies from "B" Refilling Point.	Swa.
	12		Heavy ammunition supply by pack and ammunition wagons. 1 o.r. killed & 1 o.r. wounded while delivering ammunition to 255th Bde. Enemy aircraft active over area in evening. Many bombs dropped in vicinity of camp. Heavy enemy shelling of area	Swa.
	13.14.15.		Heavy ammunition supply.	Swa.
	16		Abnormal ammunition supply. 100 pack animals lent from 23rd divisional Artillery to day. to assist in getting ammunition up. 26 o.r. attached as reinforcements from R.H.+ R.F.A. Base depot. 19 o.r. posted to Brigade. 83 LD. remounts for Div. arty. received from Remount depot. 34 allotted to D.A.C.	Swa.
	17		56 o.r. reinforcements posted to Brigades. Heavy ammunition supply. Heavy enemy shelling of area. Enemy aircraft again active at night.	Swa.
	18. 19		Heavy ammunition supply. 4 o.r. sent to 51st Army Rest Camp, Boulogne. Enemy aircraft active.	Swa.
	20		C.R.A. visits camp and inspects animals & lines. Heavy ammunition supply.	Swa.
	21		Heavy ammunition supply to gun positions.	Swa.
	22		Heavy ammunition supply to gun positions. C.R.A. + Staff. Captain visits lines.	Swa.

Army Form C. 2118.

WAR DIARY
INTELLIGENCE SUMMARY

(2)

(Erase heading not required.)

Instructions regarding War Diaries and Intelligence Summaries are contained in F.S. Regs., Part II. and the Staff Manual respectively. Title pages will be prepared in manuscript.

Place	Date	Hour	Summary of Events and Information	Remarks and references to Appendices
FIELD	1917 August 23, 24		Heavy ammunition supply. Enemy aircraft active over lines	2.w.a.
	25.		21 o.r. reinforcements attached from R.H.+R.F.A. Base depot pending disposal. Heavy ammunition supply.	2.w.a.
	26.		Heavy ammunition supply to gun position.	2.w.a.
	27.		21 o.r. reinforcements posted to Brigades. 14 o.r. reinforcements attached from No.4 Reinforcement Coy. pending disposal.	2.w.a. 2.w.a.
	28.		Heavy ammunition supply. 2 officer reinforcements from R.H.+R.F.A. Base depot, attached pending disposal.	2.w.a.
	29.		2 officer reinforcements posted – one to 235th Bde R.F.A. and one to 262 Bde R.F.A. Heavy ammunition supply.	2.w.a.
	30.		Divisional S.A.A. and grenade dump at POND COTTAGE (C.19.5.7.), (sheet 28) taken over from 11 K. Division and 1 officer + 6 o.r. sent in charge. One o.r. sent in charge of Iron Ration dump at POND COTTAGE. Heavy ammunition supply.	2.w.a. 2.w.a.
	31.		Heavy ammunition supply. 3 o.r. reinforcements attached from R.H.+R.F.A. Base Depot. Weather during month wet with intervals of dry sunny weather. Roads lines soft and transport difficult.	2.w.a.

T. W. Alexander
Major
for Lieut Colonel
Commdg. 51 D.A.C.

Vol 25

War Diary
of
51st (Highland) Divisional Ammunition Column R.F.A.
for
September, 1917

Army Form C. 2118.

WAR DIARY
INTELLIGENCE SUMMARY.
51st (Highland) Divisional Ammunition Column. R.F.A.

(Erase heading not required.)

Instructions regarding War Diaries and Intelligence Summaries are contained in F. S. Regs., Part II. and the Staff Manual respectively. Title pages will be prepared in manuscript.

Place	Date	Hour	Summary of Events and Information	Remarks and references to Appendices
FIELD	1917 SEPT. 1		D.A.C. Hd.Qrs. mounted at B.26.a (Sheet 28) in HOSPITAL FARM district. 'B' Refilling Point under charge of D.A.C. officer at H.W.L. Divisional Grenade Store at POND COTTAGE, (C.19.c).	Swan
	2.		Heavy ammunition supply. Large amount of ammunition now being sent from XVIII L C.A.P. by light railway to FUSILIER FARM. (C.W.c)	Swan
	3, 4		Heavy ammunition supply by light railway, and by wagons from 'B' Refilling Point	Swan
	5		D.A.C. camp came under shell fire. Enemy aircraft active all day over area. Several men wounded by bombs.	Swan
	6.		D.A.C. camp again under shell fire. 1 man killed and 2 wounded by a shell.	Swan
	7		Grenade Dump at POND COTTAGE struck by enemy shell and D.A.C. officer in charge burned for one hour, sustaining injuries which necessitated his evacuation to hospital. Heavy ammunition supply by light railway to FUSILIER FARM. Enemy aircraft active over camp. 1 man severely wounded and 8 men slightly wounded by bombs.	Swan
	{ 8, 9 10, 11		Main ammunition supply to FUSILIER FARM.	Swan
	12		Heavy ammunition supply to FUSILIER FARM, and by wagons to Battery Positions. Enemy aircraft again active over area. 2 or wounded in evening by bombs.	Swan
	13		Heavy ammunition supply. Enemy aircraft again active over area.	Swan

Army Form C. 2118.

WAR DIARY
INTELLIGENCE SUMMARY.
(Erase heading not required.)

Instructions regarding War Diaries and Intelligence Summaries are contained in F. S. Regs., Part II. and the Staff Manual respectively. Title pages will be prepared in manuscript.

Place	Date	Hour	Summary of Events and Information	Remarks and references to Appendices
FIELD	1917 Sept 14		Heavy ammunition supply by light railway, and by pack from D.A.C. Large number of wagons engaged in salvage work.	S.W.A.
	15		Fair ammunition supply. Enemy aircraft very active over area at night.	S.W.A.
	16		Heavy ammunition supply, and R.E. fatigue. C.R.A. Division, visited D.A.C. lines in afternoon. 1 O.R. wounded by bomb in forward area. Camp under shell fire in morning.	S.W.A.
	17/18		Heavy ammunition supply to FUSILIER FARM, and to batteries by wagons from "B" dump.	S.W.A.
	19		Heavy ammunition supply to FUSILIER FARM. Salvage in area almost completed.	S.W.A.
	20		Ammunition supply suspended during assault.	S.W.A.
	21		Heavy ammunition supply to FUSILIER FARM, and by wagons to batteries. 123 L.D. remounts arrived from PROVEN Railhead. Enemy aircraft active over area all day.	S.W.A.
	22		Enemy aircraft active in morning and at night. Heavy ammunition supply to FUSILIER FARM. 25 O.R. reinforcement attached from Base Depot, pending disposal.	S.W.A.
	23		Enemy aircraft active all day. Heavy ammunition supply to FUSILIER FARM. 25 O.R. reinforcements posted — 7 to D.A.C.	S.W.A.
	24		Heavy ammunition supply to FUSILIER FARM. Grenade dump at POND COTTAGE handed over, at 12 noon, to 11th. Division.	S.W.A.

2353 Wt W 2544/1454 700,000 5/15 D. D. & L. A.D.S.S./Forms/C. 2118.

WAR DIARY

INTELLIGENCE SUMMARY.

(Erase heading not required.)

Army Form C. 2118.

Instructions regarding War Diaries and Intelligence Summaries are contained in F. S. Regs., Part II. and the Staff Manual respectively. Title pages will be prepared in manuscript.

Place	Date	Hour	Summary of Events and Information	Remarks and references to Appendices
FIELD	1917 Sept 25		1 officer, reinforcement attached from Base Depot. D.A.C. came under orders of 11th D.A. at 12 noon. 9 o.r. reinforcements attached from Base Depot. Enemy aircraft active at night.	Swar
	26		Heavy ammunition supply to FUSILIER FARM. 1 officer, reinforcement, attached from Base Depot. C.R.A. 11th Division, visited D.A.C. in afternoon.	Swar
	27		Heavy ammunition supply. 2 officers and 9 o.r. reinforcements, posted to Brigades R.F.A. 2 o.r. killed, 1 o.r. wounded by hostile shell fire in forward area, while delivering ammunition. Enemy aircraft active at night.	Swar
	28		Heavy ammunition supply to FUSILIER FARM. 4 o.r. reinforcements, attached from Base Depot. 1 posted to D.A.C. & 3 to 85th Brigade, R.F.A.	Swar
	29		Heavy ammunition supply. Abnormal activity of enemy aircraft during night, between 8 p.m. and 2 a.m. (30th). Several hundred bombs dropped in area. About 90 animals of D.A.C. killed and wounded; No personnel.	Swar
	30		Fair ammunition supply. Considerable enemy aerial activity over lines during night. No casualties in D.A.C.	Swar
			Weather during month dry and sunny. Enemy aircraft very active specially during the latter part of the month.	Swar

J. W. Alexander Major
51 D.A.C.

CONFIDENTIAL
No 21 (A)
HIGHLAND
DIVISION.

War Diary

of

51st (Highland) Divisional Ammunition Column, RFA.

for

October, 1917.

Army Form C. 2118.

WAR DIARY
INTELLIGENCE SUMMARY
(Erase heading not required)

51st (Highland) Divisional Ammunition Column R.F.A.

Instructions regarding War Diaries and Intelligence Summaries are contained in F. S. Regs., Part II. and the Staff Manual respectively. Title pages will be prepared in manuscript.

Place	Date	Hour	Summary of Events and Information	Remarks and references to Appendices
FIELD	1917 Oct 1		D.A.C. still encamped in HOSPITAL FARM Area, at B.26.a (sheet 28). Heavy amm. supply to Brigade and FUSILIER FARM. Enemy aircraft active at night. 3 OR wounded in forward area, while on ammunition supply to gun positions.	H.B.K.
	2		Enemy aircraft active in early morning bombing. 50 OR reinforcements arrived in morning from R.H. + R.F.A. Base depot and attached to D.A.C. pending Field ammunition supply. 1 NCO and 6 men proceeded to rail rail-head to take over S.A.A. & grenade dumps. Enemy aircraft again active at night	H.B.K.
	3		Heavy ammunition supply to battery positions. Enemy aircraft active at night dropping several bombs near D.A.C. lines.	H.B.K.
	4		Heavy ammunition supply. 3 OR severely wounded & several animals killed & wounded owing to direct hit by enemy shell. 50 OR reinforcements posted to Brigades.	H.B.K.
	5		Heavy ammunition supply. 197 L.D. remounts arrived at PROVEN for 51st D.A. and detailed to various frm Brigade A.D.C.	H.B.K.
	6		Heavy ammunition supply. Enemy aircraft active towards midnight, bombing.	H.B.K.
	7		Heavy ammunition supply. Roads becoming soft and cut up owing to continuous rain. Heavy ammunition supply	H.B.K.
	8		D.A.C. took over FUSILIER FARM dumps from F.A. Division, and an officer and NCO in charge.	H.B.K.
	9		to Batteries. Transport becoming difficult. Heavy ammunition supply. Enemy aircraft active over lines at night, bombing	H.B.K.
	10		Heavy ammunition supply. Difficult transport conditions.	H.B.K.
	11		very wet and muddy. 32 OR reinforcements attached from Base depot. D.A.C. came under administration of 18th D.A.	H.B.K.
	12		Heavy ammunition supply. D.A.C. shelled by high velocity gun in afternoon. Several casualties to men and animals caused. 1 officer & 29 OR reinforcements attached from Base depot	H.B.K.
	13		Heavy ammunition supply.	H.B.K.
	14		Enemy aircraft active all day, dropping bombs. 61 OR posted to Brigades. 34 OR reinforcements arrived from Base depot. Heavy ammunition supply. 30 Reserve Park handed over to "Q" Branch XVIII Corps at	H.B.K.
	15		now and D.A.C. party rejoined D.A.C. 1 Officer & out OR proceeded to No.5 Base Remount depot CALAIS for 48 remounts. All horsed ammunition, including S.A.A. to be dumped at XVIII C.A.P. before D.A.C. moves out. Heavy amm. supply. 34 OR posted to Brigades. Enemy aircraft very active at night.	H.B.K.
	16		Heavy amm. supply.	H.B.K.
	17		1 Officer & 61 OR reinforcements arrived from Base depot	H.B.K.
	18	11 am	D.A.C. left HOSPITAL FARM and proceed by YPRES – POPERINGHE Road to HAMHOEK area, arriving about 1.30 pm. Entraining order received 2 pm.	H.B.K.
	19		Entraining of D.A.C. commenced. Echelons being entrained and despatched south in detachment, viâ Bapaume, at intervals during the day	H.B.K.
	20		Echelons completed entraining. H.Q. entrained with No 1 Co. Dn Train A.S.C. 6 OR reinforcements attached from Brookfield.	H.B.K.
	21		D.A.C. detrained at BEAUSSART (Somme) and proceeded to hutments at LOUVENCOURT. 6 OR posted to Brigade. 34 OR reinforcements attached from Base depot.	H.B.K.
	22		Cleaning of harness, wagons, equipment &c.	H.B.K.

[signature] Lt Col 51st D.A.C.

Army Form C. 2118.

WAR DIARY
INTELLIGENCE SUMMARY.
(Erase heading not required.)

Instructions regarding War Diaries and Intelligence Summaries are contained in F. S. Regs., Part II. and the Staff Manual respectively. Title pages will be prepared in manuscript.

Place	Date 1917	Hour	Summary of Events and Information	Remarks and references to Appendices
FIELD.	22 23		67 or. postes to Brigade. Bearing of horses re. provided with	MSK
	24		34 or. postes to Brigade. D.A.C. worked by LORD BUTE, who arrived from G.H.Q at 8pm aus stays overnight.	MSK
	25.		Lectures, reinforcements, postes to Brigade	MSK
	26 27 28		Bearing of horses began & continued	MSK
	29		C.R.A. inspected D.A.C. in afternoon. 18 or. reinforcements arrived from Base depot	MSK
	30		Reorganisation of D.A.C. completed + surplus men, animals + vehicles ready to sent away. 4/3 arrived sent to 252 Brigade R.F.A	MSK
	31		Bearing of horses, equipment etc. proceeded with.	MSK

trenches not during first half of month, but fairly dry during latter half.

[signature] Lt.Col.
51st D.A.C.

CONFIDENTIAL
No. 21(A)
HIGHLAND DIVISION.

WAR DIARY

OF

51st (HIGHLAND) DIVISIONAL AMMUNITION COLUMN, R.F.A.

FOR

NOVEMBER, 1914.

Army Form C. 2118.

WAR DIARY
or
INTELLIGENCE SUMMARY.

5/(Highland) Div. Ammn. Col. R.F.A.

(Erase heading not required.)

Instructions regarding War Diaries and Intelligence Summaries are contained in F. S. Regs., Part II. and the Staff Manual respectively. Title pages will be prepared in manuscript.

Place	Date 1917	Hour	Summary of Events and Information	Remarks and references to Appendices
FIELD	Nov 1		D.A.C. at LOUVENCOURT. 18 o.r. reinforcement from Base posted to Brigades. Preparations made for move.	H.A.K
	2		Continuation of preparations for move.	H.A.K
	3	8 a.m.	D.A.C. left LOUVENCOURT and proceeded via MAILLY-MAILLET – SERRE – AYETTE to BOIRY ST. MARTIN, arriving at 4 p.m.	H.A.K
	4,5		Sorting out of harness & equipment.	H.A.K
	6	6.45 a.m.	D.A.C. left rendezvous camp and proceeded via AYETTE – SERRE – MAILLY-MAILLET to LOUVENCOURT, arriving at noon.	H.A.K
	7		Sorting out and cleaning of harness, equipment etc.	H.A.K
	8		15 G.S. wagons + party sent to LECHELLE as advance party.	H.A.K
	9-13		Sorting out + cleaning harness, wagons, equipment etc.	H.A.K
	14		8 o.r. proceeded to METZ to take over S.A.A. + grenade dump there.	H.A.K
	15		1 officer and in charge of S.A.A. + grenade dump at METZ.	H.A.K
	16		Orders received direct from VI Corps R.A. to move to COURCELLES area on 17th inst. Move to be complete before 7 a.m. the following morning.	H.A.K
	17	4 p.m.	D.A.C. left LOUVENCOURT and proceeded via MAILLY-MAILLET – PUISIEUX – SERRE to COURCELLES arriving at 1 a.m. on 18th.	H.A.K
	18	4 p.m.	D.A.C. left COURCELLES area and proceeded via BAPAUME to BEAULENCOURT, arriving at 8.30 p.m.	H.A.K
	19		Sorting out + cleaning of harness &c.	H.A.K
	20	5.15 a.m.	D.A.C. left BEAULENCOURT and proceeded via BUS to LECHELLE, arriving at 8.30 a.m. 1 officer + party sent in charge of Ammunition dump in HAVRINCOURT WOOD.	H.A.K
	21	10.30 a.m.	No 2 Section, D.A.C. moved to area east of METZ on METZ – TRESCAULT road. Delivery of ammunition at the gun positions of 51st Divisional Artillery just commenced.	H.A.K
	22	9 a.m.	D.A.C. left LECHELLE and proceeded to METZ arriving at 11 a.m. Lorries delivered ammunition in limbers to Ammn dump. Heavy ammunition supply to advanced dump at FLESQUIÈRES.	H.A.K
	23		Heavy ammunition supply all day and night owing to heavy enemy counter attack.	H.A.K
	24		Heavy ammunition supply. D.A.C. came under Guards Divisional Artillery.	H.A.K
	25		Heavy ammunition supply to the Hag Line. Delivery of ammunition at the positions also proceeded with, and almost completed. 1 officer proceeds to D.A.C. from 23(A) B.E.F.R.F.	H.A.K
	26	5 a.m.	Large amount of gun ammunition arrives by motor lorry and dumped in METZ. Continuation of ammn. supply.	H.A.K
	27		Delivery of amm. at its position completed. 3 officers posted to D.A.C. from Base depot.	H.A.K
	28		Heavy ammunition supply.	H.A.K
	29		Do.	H.A.K
	30	1 p.m.	D.A.C. Lorries move back to METZ – ROMAULCOURT road, shelling during day to enemy advance on right flank. Heavy ammn supply.	H.A.K

John Robert Robertson Lieut. Colonel
Commandt 51st D.A.C.

CONFIDENTIAL.
No 71(A)
HIGHLAND DIVISION.

YA 28

War Diary
of
51st D.A.C.
for
December, 1917.

WAR DIARY
INTELLIGENCE SUMMARY

51st (Highland) Divisional Ammunition Column, RFA

Army Form C. 2118.

Place	Date 1917 Dec	Hour	Summary of Events and Information	Remarks and references to Appendices
FIELD.			Reference Map SHEET 57c	
	1.		HQ and No 3 Section in METZ-EN-COUTURE (Q.20). Sections 1 and 2 in area round ROYAULCOURT (P.10). 3 officers and parties to D.A.C. from Base Depôt.	
	2.		2 officers parties to D.A.C. from Base Depôt. Heavy ammunition supply. Heavy enemy shelling of area.	
	3.	noon	S.A.A. and Grenade Dumps at BEUGNY taken over by D.A.C. from 56th Division and 1 officer and 6 O.R. sent in charge. 6 O.R. reinforcements arrived and parties to 256 Brigade RFA.	
	4.		2 captured German 77 mm guns brought in by D.A.C. from FLESQUIERES area.	
	5,6,7, 8,9, 10.		Heavy ammunition supply. Heavy enemy shelling of area. Enemy aircraft active bombing in evening.	
	11.	2 p.m.	Heavy shelling of area all day. No 3 Section moved at 2 p.m. to BERTINCOURT (P7 and 8).	
	12.	8 a.m.	Heavy ammunition supply. Preparations for move. D.A.C. moves to new area on BAPAUME – PERONNE Road (N.H.6). Sections come down to area round Griffith Camp on BAPAUME – BANCOURT Road (H.35).	
	13		Clearing and sorting out of horses, wagons & equipment. Heavy R.E. fatigue.	
	14		No 3 Section moves to MILL CROSS area, east of BAPAUME (I.26) HQ moves to GRIFFITH Camp. Heavy wagon fatigue	
	15		Heavy wagon fatigue with R.E. Enemy aircraft active bombing area in evening. Hans foot reserving transport conditions difficult owing to slippery condition of roads.	
	16,17,18 19,20		Continuation of Hans foot making transport difficult	
	21.		Heavy wagon fatigue. 3 Officers parties from D.A.C. to Brigades RFA – 2 to 255 and 1 to 256. Hans foot continues	
	22.		Hans foot continues. Enemy aircraft active in evening.	
	23.		1 officer parties to D.A.C. from Base Depôt. Hans foot continues	
	24,25		Heavy wagon fatigue with R.E. & continuation of foot.	
	26		1 officer parties to 255th Brigade RFA. Heavy wagon fatigue. Continuation of foot.	
	27,28		Heavy wagon fatigue.	
	29.		Thaw. @ 1140 2 Indian O.R. parties to D.A.C. from General Indian Base Depôt	
	30.		Heavy wagon fatigue.	
	31		Heavy wagon fatigue. 2 officers parties to D.A.C. from Base Depôt. Heavy wagon fatigue. Thaw continues	
			Weather during month dry, with exception of month foot.	

J.M.B.... for
Capt
Lt Col.
Commanding Highland Divisional Ammn. Colmn.

Vol 29

War Diary
of
51st D.A.C.
for
January. 1918

Army Form C. 2118.

WAR DIARY
INTELLIGENCE SUMMARY.— 51st (Highland) Divisional Ammn Col. RFA

(Erase heading not required.)

Instructions regarding War Diaries and Intelligence Summaries are contained in F. S. Regs., Part II. and the Staff Manual respectively. Title pages will be prepared in manuscript.

Place	Date 1918	Hour	Summary of Events and Information	Remarks and references to Appendices
FIELD	JAN. 1		SHEET 57C	
			D.A.C. at GRIFFITH CAMP (H. 35 central). Dumps at BEUGNY & LEBUCQUIERE in charge of D.A.C. officer. Wagon fatigue suspended for the day.	Annexn.
	2		Heavy wagon fatigue. Ground very bad & slippery owing to continued frost. 2 Officers reinforcements posted from Base Depot.	Annexn.
	3		Usual wagon fatigue.	Annexn.
	4, 5		Usual fatigues, continuation of above. 16 O.R. reinforcements attached from Base.	Annexn.
	6		3 reinforcement officers posted to Brigades.	Annexn.
	7		1 Officer & 15 O.R. attached from Base depot. 31 O.R. posted to Brigades.	Annexn.
	8		Continuation of above. Heavy frost in forward area around DOIGNIES & DEMICOURT. As also ammunition is being taken down by Decauville.	Annexn.
	9, 10		Salvage work hindered by heavy falls of snow.	Annexn.
	11		Usual fatigues & continuation of salvage of ammunition.	Annexn.
	12		Heavy precautions adopted. 140 O.R. reinforcements attached from Base depot.	Annexn.
	13		1 Officer & 15 O.R. attached to P/Hrs. By RFA while engaged in salvage operation around DOIGNIES & DEMICOURT. 12 other & 51 L.D. reinforcement arrived in D.A.C. lines from No. 2 Remount Depot. ABBEVILLE.	Annexn.
	14	10 am	Remounts distributed to Brigades & D.A.C. 40 O.R. reinforcements arrives & posted to Brigade.	Annexn.
	15, 16		Usual wagon fatigue. Heavier than usual precautions observed in forces. 18 reinforcements arrived from Base depot.	Annexn.
	17		Heavy demands for wagons owing to move of 153rd Infantry Bde. to COURCELLES area.	Annexn.
	18, 19		Wagons still engaged in moving division of 153rd Infantry Bde. Salvage work hindered on 19th by very heavy enemy shell fire. 12 Lorries on reinforcements posted to D.A.C.	Annexn.
	20, 21		Usual salvage work & fatigues. Reparations for move. Contingent of equipment & ganging of wheeler.	Annexn.
	22		51st D.A. canteen at DOIGNIES handed over to 6th D.A. 1 Officer & 31 O.R. reinforcement attached from Base Depot.	Annexn.
	23		Usual fatigues. Heavy precautions.	Annexn.
	24	2 pm	51st D.A.C. moves into BAPAUME taking over camp fatigues from 6th D.A. HQ establishes at AVESNES-LES-BAPAUME. 3 O.R. posted to Bde. Heavy assault of wagons to IV Corps Q.	Annexn.
	25		Heavy wagon fatigues. Area bombed at night by enemy aircraft.	Annexn.
	26		4 Officers reinforcements attached from Base. Heavy corps fatigues involving every 2 wagon.	Annexn.
	27		Heavy wagon fatigues. Area bombed in evening.	Annexn.
	28		Heavy bombing of BAPAUME in evening. D.A.C. lost 21 animals killed & 14 wounded. 2 bombs dropped about 10 pm.	Annexn.
	29		2/Lt KF. Wagno attached to D.A.C. from 9th Reserve Bde. to assist in extra fatigues (Impoos being trained by D.A.C.) very heavy bombing of BAPAUME area in evening. D.A.C. lost 16 animals killed & 6 wounded. Quantity of stores also blown up.	Annexn.
	30, 31		Heavy fatigues. Month comparatively dry, not much frost, especially during first half.	Annexn.

Wm W___ [signature] Lt.Col.
51 D.A.C.

CONFIDENTIAL
No. 21A
HIGHLAND
DIVISION.

Vol 30

War Diary
of
51st D.A.C.
for
February, 1918.

WAR DIARY

INTELLIGENCE SUMMARY

(Erase heading not required.)

Army Form C. 2118.

Instructions regarding War Diaries and Intelligence Summaries are contained in F.S. Regs., Part II. and the Staff Manual respectively. Title pages will be prepared in manuscript.

Place	Date 1918.	Hour	Summary of Events and Information	Remarks and references to Appendices
FIELD.	FEB. 1.		REFERENCE SHEET, 57c - 1/40000	
			D.A.C. Headquarters at AVESNES-LES-BAPAUME. Rations in cellars in the town. Heavy wagon detail for fatigues in IV Corps area. 1 officer, reinforcement, attached from Base Depôt. Section of Corps stables at AVESNES-LES-BAPAUME. Kung continued daily.	R.O.R.
	2		Heavy wagon fatigues.	R.O.R.
	3		Enemy aircraft active about 2 a.m. Several bombs dropped in area. Heavy wagon details.	R.O.R.
	4		39 O.R. reinforcements attached from R.H. & R.F.A. Base Depôt. Heavy wagon fatigues.	R.O.R.
	5		Heavy wagon fatigues.	R.O.R.
	6		39 O.R. reinforcements posted to Brigades & D.A.C. - 2 to D.A.C. 2 officers posted from Base Depôt to D.A.C.	R.O.R.
	7		3 officers attached from Base Depôt.	R.O.R.
	8.	8 a.m.	20 L.D. remounts arrived at BAPAUME for 51st D.A., and distributes to Staff Captain of HQ. D.A.C. at 10.30 a.m. All the animals allotted to D.A.C. 3 officers from Base Depôt posted to D.A.C. Heavy wagon detail.	R.O.R.
	9, 10, 11, 12, 13		Heavy wagon fatigues. Preparations made for move to BANCOURT area. Farmers' canteen taken over from 6th Division. (Situation BEAUMETZ)	R.O.R.
	14	10 a.m.	51st D.A.C. moves into area occupied by 6th D.A.C. on being relieved by 25th D.A.C. H.Q. Rations 1 and 2 established at GRIFFITH CAMP, H 35 central, and S.A.A. Section at MILL CROSS. (1.27 central). All Corps fatigues handed over to 25th D.A.C. and all unhorsed amm. dumps before moving, to be taken over by 25th D.A.C. Boche gun amm. of 6th D.A.C. area.	R.O.R.
	15		Improvement of camp commenced. Harnesses and stables proceeded with. 1 Officer attaches from Base Depôt. Salvage of amm. in forward area commenced, and proceeded with daily.	R.O.R.
	16		Improving of camp continued, and protection of fields & stables against enemy aircraft proceeded with daily. Enemy aircraft active over area at night.	R.O.R.
	17		Heavy R.E. wagon fatigue clearing protection of camp &c.	R.O.R.
	18.		27 British + 12 Indian O.R. reinforcements arrived from Base Depôt. 27 white O.R. posted to Bdes & 12 Indian to D.A.C.	R.O.R.
	19.		C.R.A. inspects D.A.C. commencing with S.A.A. Section at 2.30 p.m. and concluding about 4.30. Inspection included a march past, and a general inspection of men, animals, fields &c. Enemy aircraft active in evening.	R.O.R.
	20, 21, 22, 23		Heavy wagon fatigues + salvage of amm. G.O.C. Division inspects Rifles & stalls at H 35 central on W'nt.	R.O.R.
	24.		Supply of ammunition to reinforcing and reserve Battery Positions commenced.	H.O.K.
	25		Heavy amm. supply to reserve positions of 155-156 Bdes and 293 (Army) Bde.	H.O.K.
	26	11 a.m.	S.A.A. Section left MILL CROSS and proceeded to new area at H 35 central. 2 dram personnel remained at MILL CROSS finding erection of suitable hutments in new area. Heavy supply of amm. to reserve positions.	M.S.K.
	27		Heavy amm supply.	H.O.K.
	28.		1 Mule + 14 L.D. remounts allotted to D.A.C. Heavy amm supply to reserve positions.	H.O.K.

Chittoor Roberts Lt.Col 51st D.A.C.

Vol 31

War Diary
of
51st D. A. C.
for
MARCH 1915

WAR DIARY
INTELLIGENCE SUMMARY

Army Form C. 2118.

51st (Highland) Divisional Amm. Col. RFA

(Erase heading not required.)

Place	Date 1918	Hour	Summary of Events and Information	Remarks and references to Appendices
Fues	March 1		REFERENCE SHEETS:— 57c — 1/40000 LENS II — 1/100000. DAC in FREMICOURT area. Dumps at BEUGNY & LEBUCQUIERE. Heavy supply of ammunition to reserve gun positions. Enemy aircraft active at 5am dropping bombs in area.	Annex.
	2,3,4		Continued Heavy ammunition supply, and acting as shell & empty cartridge case in forward area.	Annex.
	5		8 OR reinforcements arrives from RH & RFA Base Depot and attached to DAC. Heavy ammunition supply.	Annex.
	6		8 OR reinforcements posted to Brigades. Heavy ammunition supply and salvage work in forward area. Looking out and protection of ammunition at reinforcing gun positions.	Annex.
	7,8		Heavy ammunition supply & salvage work	Annex.
	9		Party from DAC sent up to construct new gun positions. Ammunition supply also heavy.	Annex.
	10,11,12,13		Usual salvage work and heavy supply of ammunition to reserve gun positions. Transport coy. owing to firm nature of ground.	Annex.
	14		6 Indian OR posted to DAC from Indian advanced Base Depot. Continued heavy ammunition supply.	Annex.
	15,16,17,18,19,20		Continued heavy ammunition supply, and final adjustment of ammunition in reinforcing sub manne positions in preparation for expected enemy attack.	Annex.
	21		Enemy bombardment of exceptional severity commenced about 4.30 am destroying telephonic communication between DAC & HQ Divisional Artillery. Area around DAC heavily bombarded with heavy shells all forenoon. All ammunition supply and salvage work suspended. DAC Coo HQ moves to THILLOY area at midnight.	Annex.
	22	6am	HQ DAC proceed to join sections arriving at THILLOY at 8 am. It officers and 20 OR of DAC attaches to Brigades RFA for Suty. 142 OR reinforcements arrives from Base and posted to 255, 256 & 293 Brigades at once. Heavy ammunition supply to positions (around BEUGNY). BEUGNY and LEBUCQUIERE Dumps evacuated in evening and dumps established on BAPAUME — PERONNE Road at N.H.t. ans at N.2.a. on BAPAUME — LA BARQUE Road with DAC officers in charge. 17 guns (18pr & 4.5) drawn from Ordnance, ALBERT, and delivered to Batteries at night. Heavy issue of spare parts, springs etc. BAPAUME heavily shelled all day, and district bombed at night.	
	23		Very heavy ammunition supply to Battery positions in FREMICOURT (now FRIMICOURT area) Enemy shelling now made heavily all day. Heavy shelling necessitated evacuation of dumps at N.H.t. in afternoon. DAC all out in supplying gun ammunition and S.A.A. No 3 Section being reserved to supply of SAA only. Enemy aircraft active in evening bombing, but no damage done in DAC lines.	Annex.
	24		Heavy ammunition supply. Train load of gun ammunition arrives at LA BARQUE Station about 11 am and unloaded by DAC. 18 lorry loads of ammunition also arrived during day, and dumped on WARLENCOURT Road, close to its junction with the BAPAUME — ALBERT Road, being issued as soon as dumped. Issue from LA BARQUE Station also extremely heavy and continued till supply no exhausted. DAC	Annex.

Army Form C. 2118.

WAR DIARY
of
INTELLIGENCE SUMMARY: 51st (Highland) Divisional Ammunition Column
(Erase heading not required.)

Instructions regarding War Diaries and Intelligence Summaries are contained in F. S. Regs., Part II. and the Staff Manual respectively. Title pages will be prepared in manuscript.

Place	Date 1918	Hour	Summary of Events and Information	Remarks and references to Appendices
	March 24	(cont)	Sections moved at 2pm to IRLES area & HQ took up position on WARLENCOURT Road, close to Dumps	
	25		HQ Section moved 1 and 2 moved to MAILLY MAILLET arriving there at 10 am. S.A.A. Section moved to FORCEVILLE, under orders of Division "Q", being temporarily detached from D.A.C. D.A.C. drew 9 guns from SAILLY AU-BOIS and delivered these to 255 & 256 Bdes at night. Several damaged guns handed over to Dos for return to Ordnance. Sudden orders received in afternoon for D.A.C. (less S.A.A. Section) to move to FONQUEVILLERS D.A.C. accordingly left MAILLY at 6pm and reached FONQUEVILLERS about 2am. (26th)	Johnson
	26	6 am	D.A.C. (less S.A.A. Section) moves from FONQUEVILLERS to BIENVILLERS. Sudden orders received at 10 am to trek north from BIENVILLERS to SAULTY (on DOULLENS-ARRAS Road). D.A.C. moves at once and arrives at SAULTY at 5pm after a hard march. Owing to improved situation the Column returned to BIENVILLERS in evening, arriving at 9.30 pm. Enemy aircraft active over SAULTY area, and several bombs dropped, in evening.	Johnson
	27.		No orders to move received, and advantage taken of short respite to overhaul wagons, harness &c, and to groom animals carefully.	Johnson
	28	11 am	Orders received to continue move. D.A.C. left BIENVILLERS at 2pm and proceeded via DOULLENS to LE SOUICH, arriving at 12 midnight. S.A.A. Section rejoins Column there. Orders received at 1 am to continue move. All ammunition boxes & unboxed dumped at LE SOUICH by 6pm o.b.o.	Johnson
	29	12 noon	D.A.C. left LE SOUICH and proceeded via CONCHY-SUR-CANCHE to GALAMETZ district, arriving at 6pm.	Johnson
	30.		No orders received to move. Sorting out of harness, equipment &c. Orders received at 5pm for move the following day.	Johnson
	31.		D.A.C. left GALAMETZ at 10 a.m. and proceeded via LINZEUX, RAMECOURT to HERNICOURT and WAVRANS, arriving at 3pm.	Johnson
			Roads as a whole dry, & transport easy. Last 10 days very strenuous, and taxed animals and men.	Johnson

Willison
Lieut. Colonel.
Commdg. 51st (Highland) Div. Ammn. Col.

51st Divisional Artillery

WAR DIARY

51st DIVISIONAL AMMUNITION COLUMN R.F.A.

APRIL 1918

Vol 32

War Diary
of
51st D.A.C
for
April, 1918.

WAR DIARY
INTELLIGENCE SUMMARY

Army Form C. 2118.

51st (Highland) Divisional Ammunition Column R.F.A.

Place	Date 1918	Hour	Summary of Events and Information	Remarks and references to Appendices
FIELD			REFERENCE SHEETS:- LENS 11 HAZEBROUCK 5A.	
	April 1		51st D.A.C. in process of trekking from SOMME area to BÉTHUNE area. Left WAVRANS and HERNECOURT (S. of POL area) at 7.30 a.m. and proceeded via ST. POL and HOUDAIN to GONNEHEM (HQ 1 and 2) and VENDIN-LEZ-BÉTHUNE (3), arriving about 6 p.m.	Appendix
	2		D.A.C. failed to establish in gun ammunition at dump at VERQUIGNEUL (S.E. of BÉTHUNE) on authority from H.Q. Div. Arty. Indents submitted to replace deficiencies in men, horses & equipment entailed by retirement from BAPAUME area, these deficiencies being, however, very small in the case of the D.A.C.	Appendix
	3		Sorting out and cleaning of harness and equipment. Orders received at 11 p.m. for move the following day.	Appendix
	4	12 noon	D.A.C. left GONNEHEM and VENDIN-LEZ-BÉTHUNE and proceeded via LILLERS to NEDON (HQ 1.2) and NEDONCHEL (3) arriving about 5 p.m.	Appendix
	5,6,7,8		Cleaning up of billets in NEDON and NEDONCHEL which were in a dirty condition. Rest draw from LILLERS laid on floors. Overhaul of equipment &c. 90 on reinforcements attached from R.H. and R.F.A. Base depot pending posting in the Divisional Artillery. Some ammunition supplied to Brigades for calibration purposes. Instructions received to detail parties for rifle practice on rifle range near NEDON, commencing the following day.	Appendix
	9		Rifle practice on rifle range near NEDON. Three lorries had to be withdrawn on the receipt of sudden orders. Parties sent off to rifle range at intervals. These, however, were driven in by the enemy. Preparations being rapidly completed, the D.A.C. left NEDON and NEDONCHEL at 2 p.m. H.Q. & Section 1 and 2 proceeded via LILLERS to LES AMUSOIRES (about midway between ROBECQ and ST VENANT) arriving about 11 p.m. S.A.A. moved to L'ÉCLÈME (5 kilos south of ST VENANT) under orders of 51st Division. 'Q' Artillery Brigade went right into action and ammunition supply very heavy. D.A.C. refilling from dump on ROBECQ – ST VENANT Road. Area shelled all night with dropped H.E. 6. 6" Newton T.M.	Appendix
	10		Ammunition supply continued very heavy, day and night, and involving all wagons in D.A.C. arrived at D.A.C. lines at night for T.M. Batteries.	
	11		Situation necessitated the occupation of LES AMUSOIRES by lorry wagon lines, and withdrawal of D.A.C. across the AIRE – LA BASSÉE Canal to field between BUSNES and the canal. The presence of numerous refugees on the roads caused some congestion at points where possible assistance was given to them, especially in the case of old women who were overcome by their burdens and the heat of the day. Ammunition supply still very heavy and imposing a considerable strain on men and animals. Enemy shelling heavily in neighbourhood of dump.	1 o'clock
	12	6 am	Heavy ammunition supply to positions. Sudden orders received at 7 AM to withdraw behind BUSNES owing to rapid advance near CALONNE. Roads very congested all D.A.C. wagons not engaged in ammunition supply moved out at 8:30 A.M. to HAM area. HQ being established at LE CORNET BOURDOIS. An ammunition Refilling Point opened at HAM, and large consignments of ammunition dumped there by lorry during afternoon & evening; 2 + 5 How ammunition also dumped at H.Q. D.A.C. now "all out" in ammunition supply. 51st T.M. Personnel now became attached to D.A.C. About 12 noon a party of 2 officers + 30 or from T.M's went up with rifles and Lewis Guns to defend the canal bridge pending arrival of reinforcing infantry. Situation became more normal in evening and 2 T.M. wagons sent up at night with a party of T.M. men under a D.A.C. officer to bring back the 6 Newton mortars from LES AMUSOIRES, this being successfully accomplished.	A.S.C.
	13		HQ D.A.C. moved along LE CORNET BOURDOIS – MANQUEVILLE Road to point beside field crossing. Party sent to draw	A.S.C.

Arthur Whitton Lieut 51.D.A.C.

WAR DIARY
or
INTELLIGENCE SUMMARY.
(Erase heading not required.)

Army Form C. 2118.

51st (Highland) Divisional Ammunition Column R.F.A.

Place	Date 1918	Hour	Summary of Events and Information	Remarks and references to Appendices
FIELD	Apr. 13		75 L.D. remounts from MARLES-LEZ-MINES in afternoon, these remounts being distributed on arrival to 255 and 256 Brigade R.F.A.	A.S.K
	14		Heavy ammunition supply. D.A.C. party at Canal Bank reported unit on being relieved	A.S.K
	15		Ammunition supply still heavy. 1 O.R. killed & 3 horses wounded by M.G. fire on ROBECQ – CALONNE Roads while delivering amn. to gun positions.	A.S.K
	16		2 officers posted to D.A.C. as reinforcements from R.H. and R.F.A. Basedepot	A.S.K
	17		1 D.A.C. officer posted to 256 Brigade R.F.A.	A.S.K
	18		1 D.A.C. officer posted to 255 Brigade R.F.A. Ammunition supply normal. Work of collecting ammunition from dumps on ROBECQ – ST VENANT Road commenced and continued nightly, this ammunition being transported to dump on BUSNES – LILLERS road. All empties taken to LAMBRES Railhead.	A.S.K
	19 20 21 22		Normal amn. supply to battery positions. Roads hard and dry and transport conditions good. Enemy bombarding LILLERS at frequent intervals with H.V. guns.	A.S.K
	23		New Divisional Amn. Refilling Point established at Cross Roads LE CORNET BOURDOIS. Dump at HAM being moved ammunition supply fairly heavy to positions. 9 officers attached to D.A.C. from R.H. and R.F.A. Base depot	A.S.K
	24		Normal amn. supply. 2 reinforcement officers posted to each of 255 and 256 Brigades R.A.	A.S.K
	25		R.A. Canteen opened in LA PERRIÈRE (S.W. of ST VENANT, near Canal Bank). Enemy bombarding LILLERS at intervals during afternoon. Normal ammunition supply.	A.S.K
	26		Normal amn. supply.	A.S.K
	27		2 Officer reinforcements attached from R.H. and R.F.A. Basedepôt. Normal amn. supply	A.S.K
	28		G.O.C. 51st Division inspected lines of D.A.C. in afternoon. Fairly heavy ammunition supply	A.S.K
	29		Fair amn. supply	A.S.K
	30		Normal amn. supply	A.S.K
			Weather during month dry on the whole and roads in good condition, which greatly decreased the difficulties of an abnormal ammunition supply.	A.S.K

Ch. Hutton Ltd Col.
51st D.A.C.

No 33

War Diary
of
51st S.A.C.
for
May 1918

Army Form C. 2118.

WAR DIARY
or
INTELLIGENCE SUMMARY.
(Erase heading not required.)

Instructions regarding War Diaries and Intelligence Summaries are contained in F. S. Regs., Part II. and the Staff Manual respectively. Title pages will be prepared in manuscript.

Place	Date	Hour	Summary of Events and Information	Remarks and references to Appendices
			REFERENCE SHEET 36 A. — 1/100000	
FIELD	1918 MAY 1		HQ DAC established at level crossing at O34c. Nos 1, 2 & 3 Sections situated in HAM-EN-ARTOIS district. ARP with DAC officer i/c situated at O3d at B.6. on western outskirt of LE CORNET BOURDOIS. 80 or. anglos to reorganized establishment of DAC, departed to First Army R.A. Reinforcement Camp.	1-8-K
	2-3		Heavy gun and T.M. ammunition supply to positions.	1-3 K
	4		S.A.A. Section DAC came under orders of 51st Division 'Q' and moved with 51st Divisional Infantry to new area near ARRAS. Heavy ammunition supply to positions.	1-3 K
	5		S.A.A. Section billets outside MARŒUIL in divisional area.	1-3 K
	6-7		Rain. ammunition supply to positions. Enemy shelling LILLERS with HE during afternoon. Cleaning and overhaul of wagons, harness & proceeded with.	1-3 R
	8		444 or reinforcements reported from First Army R.A. Reinforcement camp and posted to 256 and 256 Bde RFA. 1 officer posted to S.A.A. Section from Base Depot.	1-3 R
	9		Heavy ammunition supply to Bdes. Roads hard & transport easy. 31 Indian or. posted to DAC from Indian Advanced Base Depot	1-3 R
	10-11-12		Heavy ammunition supply. continued overhaul of wagons, harness & equipment	1-13 R
	13		Enemy shelled area with H.E. at intervals during day. Enemy aircraft active at night dropping bombs in area.	1-13 R

Philip Roberton Lt Col.
51st D.A.C.

WAR DIARY
INTELLIGENCE SUMMARY.

Army Form C. 2118.

Place	Date	Hour	Summary of Events and Information	Remarks and references to Appendices
FIELD	1918. MAY 14.15.16 17.18		Heavy ammunition supply to positions. Enemy aircraft active over area, commencing each night about 10 p.m.	A.15/C
	19		15 O.R. reinforcements attached from First Army R.A. Reinforcement Camp. E.A. active in evening. Several bombs dropped near section lines, and 1 O.R. wounded.	A.15/C
	20		Enemy aircraft again active in early morning. 1 officer & 2 O.R. wounded by M.G. fire.	A.15/C
	21		Heavy ammunition supply – both gun and T.M. Enemy aircraft active at night, & several bombs dropped near H.Q.	A.15/C
	22		DAC came under orders of 4th D.A., XIII Corps, and moved to new area at 10 a.m. H.Q. established in chateau in wood at western outskirts of LILLERS; No 1 Section at ALLOUAGNE (C.12.d.3&5). No 2 Section at MENSECQ (V.22.b & d. [3&9]). Ammunition dumps taken over at U.11.d.8.8 (PARK DUMP) & V.26.a.8.7. (LE TAILLY).	A.15/C
	23-24 -25.		Enemy shelled H.Q. chateau grounds at intervals, commencing usually about 6.20 a.m. daily.	A.15/C
	26		Enemy bombarded chateau grounds & surrounding area continuously during day, at intervals of from 10 to 20 minutes, becoming more intense in evening and lasting all night.	A.15/C
	27.		Heavy bombardment continued during morning & H.Q. left chateau at 11 a.m. Proceeded	A.15/C

Charles .... Lt.Col.
51st D.A.C.

Army Form C. 2118.

WAR DIARY
or
INTELLIGENCE SUMMARY.
(Erase heading not required.)

(3)

Instructions regarding War Diaries and Intelligence Summaries are contained in F. S. Regs., Part II. and the Staff Manual respectively. Title pages will be prepared in manuscript.

Place	Date	Hour	Summary of Events and Information	Remarks and references to Appendices
FIELD	1918 MAY 27.		to MENSECQ, arriving at 12.30 pm. Shelling continued till 3 pm.	1st K
	28.		4 Enemy aircraft came over camp at 5.30 pm. & dropped aerial bombs in vicinity. No damage done to camp. District bombarded with shrapnel for about an hour, shortly after. No.1 Section had 2 Bombs dropped near lines. Casualties 1 Horse Killed & 7 wounded.	1st K
	29-30. 31		Heavy ammunition supply. Enemy aircraft active nightly, commencing about 10 pm. LILLERS Railhead shelled at frequent intervals.	1st K
			Weather during month dry and warm. Enemy aircraft active during latter half.	1st K

WWhitson Lt. Col.
5.16. D.A.C.

2353 Wt. W2544/1454 700,000 5/15 D.D. & L. A.D.S.S./Forms/C. 2118.

51st (H) DIVISIONAL AMMUNITION COLUMN, R.F.A.

War Diary
51st D.A.C.
for
June, 1918

WAR DIARY
INTELLIGENCE SUMMARY

(Erase heading not required.)

Army Form C. 2118.

Instructions regarding War Diaries and Intelligence Summaries are contained in F. S. Regs., Part II. and the Staff Manual respectively. Title pages will be prepared in manuscript.

51st (H) DIVISIONAL AMMUNITION COLUMN, R.F.A.

No. ....
Date ....

Place	Date 1918	Hour	Summary of Events and Information	Remarks and references to Appendices
			REFERENCE SHEETS:- HAZEBROUCK 5A - 1/100000 LENS 11 D.	
FIELD	JUNE. 1		51st D.A.C. (less S.A.A. Section) billets in LILLERS area. H.Q. and No. 2 Section at MENSECQ, No. 1 Section at ALLOUAGNE. S.A.A Section establishes on BRAY-MAROEUIL Road under orders of 51st Division 'Q' and engaged in R.E. fatigues. S.A.A. and Grenade Dumps on ROCLINCOURT - THELUS Road under charge of D.A.C. officer. Fair ammunition supply to Batteries. 1st O.R. reinforcements arrived at MENSECQ and posted to Brigades.	A.S.K.
	2, 3, 4		Moderate ammunition supply to batteries. Sorting out of harness wagons &c in preparation for move to 51st Divisional area.	A.S.K.
	5	7 a.m.	51st D.A.C. (less S.A.A. Section) moves from MENSECQ and ALLOUAGNE. H.Q. and No. 2 Section proceeded via HOUDAIN, REBREUVE, CAUCHIN L'EGAL and ESTRÉE CAUCHIE to CAMBLAIN L'ABBÉ. No. 1 Section proceeded via LOZINGHEM, BRUAY, HAILLICOURT, BARLIN & BOUVIGNY - BOYEFFLES, but owing to lack of accommodation here, moved on to BOYEFFLES. No gun am supply as Brigades took in rest area.	A.S.K.
	6	10 a.m.	51st D.A.C. (less S.A.A. Section) inspected by G.O.C. R.A. First Army, commencing with No. 2 Section +HQ. and concluding with No. 1 Section.	A.S.K.
	7	4.30 p.m.	51st D.A.C. (less S.A.A. Section) inspected by G.O.C. First Army. 51st O.R. reinforcements arrives from First Army R.A. Reinforcement Camp and posted to Brigades.	A.S.K.
	8		1 officer & 31 O.R. despatched to No 4 Base Remount Depot to bring back 58 remounts.	A.S.K.
	9		Grenade dump moved back to ECURIE SIDING	A.S.K.

Nulton Lt Col.

Army Form C. 2118.

WAR DIARY
or
INTELLIGENCE SUMMARY.
(Erase heading not required.)

51st (H) DIVISIONAL AMMUNITION COLUMN, R.F.A.

Place	Date 1918	Hour	Summary of Events and Information	Remarks and references to Appendices
FIELD	June 10/11/12		Sorting out & cleaning of harness &c, special advantage being taken of rest to improve condition of animals.	ItsK
	13.	5 pm	Remounts arrives from BOULOGNE and distributes immediately by Staff Captain R.A. 51st Division. DAC allotted 3 riders & 9 L.D.	ItsK.
	14.15		Cleaning of harness, wagons, animals & equipment and improvement of camp.	ItsK
	16.		Intimation received that, owing to scarcity of L.D. the establishment of DAC is reduced by 72 L.D. & 36 drivers. DAC instructed to prepare to send surplus drivers & L.D. to Base on short notice.	ItsK.
	17		Usual fatigues.	ItsK
	18	12 noon	TIMBER STACK A.R.P. near MADAGASCAR CORNER taken over from 15th D.A.C.	ItsK.
	19		Epidemic of sickness broke out in HQ and No 2 Section — this sickness being locally termed "three day fever." Enemy aircraft active at night.	ItsK
	20/21		Preparations for move to BRAY- MARŒUIL area. Epidemic spreading in HQ and No 2 Section.	ItsK
	22	1.30 pm	51st DAC (less SAA Section) moves via MONT ST ELOI to BRAY- MARŒUIL Road, HQ. being established beside SAA. Section. Many sick cases had to be left behind in hospital by HQ & No 2 Section.	ItsK
	23/24/25		Epidemic still spreading in HQ and No 2 Section, involving greater part of personnel. All ammunition taken up to batteries by Light Railway — which relieves DAC. of much work during this time.	ItsK.

Andrew Johnston Lt Col.

Army Form C. 2118.

WAR DIARY
INTELLIGENCE SUMMARY.
(Erase heading not required.)

51st (H) DIVISIONAL
AMMUNITION COLUMN,
R.F.A.

Place	Date 1918	Hour	Summary of Events and Information	Remarks and references to Appendices
FIELD	June 26, 27		Epidemic spreading to No.1 Section & S.A.A. Section and seriously affecting the work of the Unit.	175 K.
	28, 29		Sickness epidemic beginning to die out in H.Q. and No.2 Section, but spreading in No.1 and S.A.A. Sections. Enemy aircraft slightly active over area at night dropping bombs. No damage done in D.A.C. lines.	175 K.
			Greater part of personnel (both British & Indian) of No.1 and S.A.A. Sections now affected with "Three-day fever." Sickness dying out in H.Q. and No.2 Section	175 K.
	30		Weather during month dry and warm, with infrequent showers. Roads and lines consequently hard and dry and transport conditions excellent. Working efficiency of Unit greatly affected during latter half of month by epidemic of sickness which spread gradually over the whole Column, and which appears to be prevalent in most units of the Division.	175 K.

Mathieson Lt Col
51st D.A.C.

Divisional Artillery

51st (Highland) Division

51st DIVISIONAL AMMUNITION COLUMN

JULY, 1918.

Army Form C. 2118

WAR DIARY
—or—
INTELLIGENCE SUMMARY.
(Erase heading not required.)

51st (H) DIVISIONAL AMMUNITION COLUMN, R.F.A.

No.............
Date...........

Instructions regarding War Diaries and Intelligence Summaries are contained in F. S. Regs., Part II. and the Staff Manual respectively. Title pages will be prepared in manuscript.

Place	Date 1918	Hour	Summary of Events and Information	Remarks and references to Appendices
Field	July 1		51st D.A.C. established on BRAY-MAREUIL Road in ARRAS district. Ammunition Refilling Point under charge of D.A.C. officer near MADAGASCAR CORNER, and S.A.A. & Grenade Dump at ECURIE being also under administration of D.A.C. Influenza epidemic now confined to Sections 1 and 3, involving greater part of these Sections. Enemy aircraft active about 11 p.m. dropping bombs in area.	Annex.
	2		Overhauling of wagons, saddlery &c. & usual fatigues	Annex.
	3	5 pm.	CRA visited D.A.C. on return from 2 month sick leave.	Annex.
	4		1 officer + 3 reinforcement attached from 1st Army R.A. Reinforcement Camp.	Annex.
	5		Reinforcement officer posted to D.A.C., 3 or to 255 Brigade RFA	Annex
	6	8 am	22 drivers & 48 animals surplus to re-organized establishment of D.A.C. despatched to No 4 Base Remount Depot BOULOGNE, the men to be subsequently sent to 1st Army R.A. Reinforcement Camp.	Annex.
	7, 8, 9		Overhaul & cleaning of animals, wagons &c. Influenza epidemic dying out.	Annex
	10		906 ut. Canadian Division & CRA 51st Division visited D.A.C.	Annex
	11	1 pm	Indian personnel of unit inspected by Lt. Gen Sir E. LOCKE-ELLIOTT, KCB, DSO, Military Adviser, Indian Army. Preparations made for move to training area west of ST. POL.	Annex.
	12	2.30 pm	CRA visited DAC. Considerable activity of enemy aircraft about 11.30 pm. bomb dropping & machine gunning.	Annex
	13	6 pm.	Final preparations made for move at midnight to ST. POL. area; this move was however cancelled at 6 pm. and orders received at 11 pm for DAC (less SAA Section) to move to LA COMTE the following morning. TIMBER STACK A.R.P. + Grenade Dump handed over to 4th Canadian DAC at noon. & dump personnel rejoined D.A.C.	Annex.
	14	9.30 am	DAC (less SAA Section) moved via MONT-ST-ELOI - ESTREE - CAUCHIE & LA COMTE arriving at 3 pm. Entraining orders received at 8.30 pm. & preparations at once made for long railway journey.	Annex.
	15		51st D.A.C. entrained in detachments with detachments of Brigade RFA & Divisional Train A.S.C. (HQ entraining at PERNES, Nos 1 and 2 Sections at PERNES-BRIAS & SAA Section at TINQUES) and proceeded South via ST POL, HESDIN, MONTREUIL, NOYELLES-SUR-MER, ABBEVILLE, PONTOISE, ST CYR, VERSAILLES, ORLY, LONGUEVILLE, to detraining points at PONT-S/SEINE, NOGENT-S/SEINE, FONTAINE-DENIS to LENHARREE (MARNE) where the DAC concentrated.	Annex.
	16			
	17			
	18		On detraining, detachments proceeded by road via DENIS to move to fixed area. SAA Section moved at 6 pm. & H.Q. concentration of column completed and orders received at noon to move to fixed area. SAA Section moved at 6 pm. & H.Q. Nos 1 and 2 Sections at 7 pm. via VERTUS & MAREUIL to point between AY & EPERNAY, on canal track, arriving about 6 am on	Annex.
	19			
	20		Ammunition Dumps taken over by DAC at NANTEUIL & GERMAINE. Division in conjunction with 62nd Division & French, attacked at 8 am. and all available ammunition wagons in DAC engaged in transporting ammunition from GERMAINE to NANTEUIL to supply the batteries of the Divisional Artillery coming into action. SAA Section moved at 11 am. via DIZY-MAGENTA to point in wood near ST. IMOGES. Enemy shelled EPERNAY all day. HQ. Nos 1 and 2 Sections moved at 8.15 pm via DIZY, up steep hill to point in wood 2 kilometres north of HAUTVILLERS, arriving at midnight.	
	21, 22, 23		Heavy ammunition supply to NANTEUIL dump. Enemy shelling district at intervals.	Annex.
	24		Heavy ammunition supply. Enemy spread an extremely heavy fire on positions in wood, in front of DAC lines commencing at 9 H.5 pm. and lasting about half an hour. 2 or killed + 4 wounded in No. 2 Section, & several animals wounded.	Annex.
	25		Enemy aircraft dropped bomb on area about midnight.	Annex.
	26		NANTEUIL dump withdrawn to DAC lines about noon. HQ. No 1 & 2 Sections moved at 4.30 pm via ST. IMOGES to point in wood near GERMAINE. Enemy aircraft active at night dropping bombs & machine gunning roads. 1 or died of wounds received 24th	Annex
	27		SAA Section shelled during night. 3 or. slightly wounded	Annex.
	28		ARP established under DAC officer on NANTEUIL-POURCY Road & DAC echelon dumps here during afternoon. HQ, No 1 & 2 Sections moved at 4.30 pm via ST. IMOGES to point in wood & at 2 pm via NANTEUIL to point midway on NANTEUIL-POURCY Road, near dump.	Annex Annex

WAR DIARY

or

INTELLIGENCE SUMMARY.

(Erase heading not required.)

Army Form C. 2118.

51st (H) DIVISIONAL AMMUNITION COLUMN, R.F.A.

No..........
Date..........

Instructions regarding War Diaries and Intelligence Summaries are contained in F. S. Regs., Part II. and the Staff Manual respectively. Title pages will be prepared in manuscript.

Place	Date 1918	Hour	Summary of Events and Information	Remarks and references to Appendices
Field	July 29	9 am	Enemy aircraft active over area. Ammunition Dump near HAUTVILLERS run out/personnel of rest dump rejoined D.A.C. Salvage of cartridge cases in area being proceeded with, prior to the divisions departure.	Appces.
	30		Continuation of salvage of empty brass cartridge cases. Ammunition at dump at NANTEUIL- POURCY being boxed & transported to EPERNINE by lorry the dump being cleared by 10 pm. Preparations made for train journey, on receipt of entraining orders.	Appces.
	31		Three entraining stations allotted to D.A.C. — EPERNAY, AVIZES, & VERTUS. D.A.C. commenced entraining at EPERNAY & AVIZES. Detachment of No 1 Section departed from EPERNAY at 3 pm & 7 pm & Section & No 2 Section leaving AVIZES at 11.30 pm. Each detachment accompanied a Battery of the divisional artillery. Ammunition echelons travelled free.	Appces.
			Weather during month dry with rain at intervals.	

Charles Johnston
Lt. Col.
Commanding Highland Divisional Ammn. Colmn.

9836

War Diary
of
51st A.S.C.
for
August 1918

WAR DIARY or INTELLIGENCE SUMMARY

Army Form C. 2118.

Place	Date 1918.	Hour	Summary of Events and Information	Remarks and references to Appendices
Field	Aug. 1		51st DAC in the process of entraining in detachments with batteries of the Div Artillery at EPERNAY, AVIZES, VERTUS & FÈRE CHAMPENOISE (MARNE) for journey from Fifth French Army to First British Army. Route via NOYON-LE SEC, PONTOISE, US, CHARS, GIZORS, SERQUEUX, SALEUX thence west of AMIENS — CANDAS to detraining stations at PERNES, BRIAS, CALONNE, thence trekking to FREVIN CAPELLE area. Concentration of DAC completed at 3 pm on 7th by arrival of last detachment of SAA section.	T.G.1
	2			
	3			
	4		Section located at CAPELLE-FERMONT.	
	5	6 pm	137 BR reinforcements arrived from First Army RA	T.G.3
	6	4.30 pm	7 officers reinforcements arrived, posted to Bdes & DAC. Enemy aircraft active over area at 11.30 pm. Bomb dropping.	
	7-8		Sorting out and clearing of equipment &c. and conditioning of animals, also being continued daily during this week.	
	9	4 pm	73 OR Reinforcements arrived from First Army RA Reinforcement Camp posted to Bdes RFA	
	10		8 OR reinforcements (artificers) posted from First Army RA R.C.	
	11-12		Usual fatigues & training programme - riding, driving, physical drill &. EA. active at 11 pm.	
	13		Warning Order received. Preparations commenced for move into the line. EA very active about midnight.	
	14		EA again active at night.	
	15	12 noon	TIMBER STACK ARP near MADAGASCAR CORNER taken over from 52nd DAC. 51st DAC moves at 4.30 pm via ACQ & ECOURES to lines & billets. Billets meant to be 52nd DAC on BRAY-MAROEUIL ROAD. HQ established with SAA section in HUTS near MAROEUIL. EA active at 11 pm	
	16	12 noon	SAA & Grenade Dump at ÉCURIE SIDING (HIGHLAND DUMP) taken over from 52nd DAC. Enemy shelled area at night with H.V. guns.	
	17	Do	REECE SPUR DUMP (SAA) at CG 9 b 2.3. (5/8) taken over from 57 DOW.	
	18		Sorting out of equipment & clearing of lines & billets.	
	19		Heavy amm supply to new Brigade positions at H.13.a.9.3 east of railway near ATHIES. DAC echelon sent up at 7 pm (unboxed) and pack animals transported the amm from dump across country to positions.	
	20		EA active at 11.30 pm.	
	21			
	22		Heavy amm supply to positions at H.13.d. continued. DAC again sending up free echelon. EA very active all night.	
	23		Heavy enemy bomb being dropped close to camp. 3.a. war active all night. Camp occupied by HQ & SAA Section bombarded at 9.45 am by H.V. guns. Shelling lasting about 15 minutes and several shells falling close up to Hut stables. No damage done. 17 OR reinforcements arrived at 10.30 am from First Army RA Reinforcement Camp and posted to Bdes. Filling up of positions at H.13.d. continued at night, the amm now being taken up by Light railway & packed to positions by DAC. Enemy shelled lines again about 11 pm, 1 OR wounded at time killed.	
	24		Filling up of positions at H.13.d. completed. No enemy fire taken on the charge of 51 DAC.	
	25		Enemy shelled vicinity of camp about midnight. No damage done.	
	26		Free DAC echelon sent up to Bdes & vicinity of our Arty at night. Enemy again shelled vicinity of camp at intervals during night.	
	27	8 am	51st DAC moved via ANZIN to point near MADAGASCAR CORNER. Heavy amm supply to Bty positions in evening.	
	28		Heavy amm supply to Bdes.	
	29	12 noon	TIMBER STACK Dump handed over to 8th Division. New Main dump now in St NICOLAS. who advanced Refilling Point east of BLANGY. DAC engaged at night in transporting amm from rear to forward Bty positions.	
	30	12 noon	"HIGHLAND" DUMP handed over to 8th Division. Salvage of empties commenced at various positions east of ROCLINCOURT.	
	31		Salvage of empty cartridge cases continued.	
			Weather during month dry &warm, with intervals of rain, especially in latter part.	

John W...... Lt. Col.
51 D.A.C.

51st (H) DIVISIONAL
AMMUNITION COLUMN,
R.F.A.
No.
Date 30.9.18

Vol 37

War Diary
of
51st D.A.C.
for
September, 1918

WAR DIARY
or
INTELLIGENCE SUMMARY.
(Erase heading not required.)

Army Form C. 2118.

51st (H) DIVISIONAL AMMUNITION COLUMN, R.F.A.

Place	Date 1918	Hour	Summary of Events and Information	Remarks and references to Appendices
Field	Sep. 1.		51st DAC located near MADAGASCAR CORNER (A.26.c. S1.B). ARP at ST NICOLAS, under DAC officer, with advanced Refilling Point East of BLANGY (M.13.b). SAA & Grenade dump at ECURIE SIDING, also under administration of DAC. Taking of ammunition & cartridge cases continued daily, these being dumped at convenient spots near Light Railway. Wagon fatigue with RE & Infantry Brigades.	1-M.R.
	2.		Road wagon fatigue, relining of B Smoke to batterie positions. Enemy aircraft active over area at 11 p.m.	M.V.R.
	3.		Wagon fatigue continued to 255 Bde. to move guns & ammunition up to new positions in FAMPOUX area.	M-V.R.
	4.		Road salvage operations and wagon fatigued.	
	5.		Ammunition supply at night to 255 and 256 Brigades. E.A. active at night.	M-V.R M-V.R
	6.		Road salvage work & fatigues	M-V.R
	7.	9 pm	33 D.A.m. of arrived as reinforcements from Indian RA advanced Bracedept, reports to Section of DAC.	M-2
	8.		Road salvage work.	M-2
	9.		Large quantity of smoke & chemical shell also from positions in front of railway embankment near ATHIES and returned to MAIN DUMP.	M-V.R
	10 11 12.		Road salvage operations.	M-V.R M-V.R
	13.	1.30 pm	Operation orders received & preparations made for move. 51st D.A.C. on being relieved by 49th DAC. 30 G. Wagons & teams detached to 50T DAC at ARRAS for storage of ammunition. 51 DAC moved via ANZIN - MONT-ST-ELOI to FREVIN CAPELLE (HQ, 2 Tpm) + AGNIERES(1) 32 Br. reinforcements arrived from First Army RA Reinforcement camp posted to Brigades.	M-V.R F-M
	14 15 16 17 18		Training programme carried out — riding and driving drill &c. advantage also taken of brief not to improve conditions of animals, wagons saddlery & equipment. Lectures to officers DA & CRA in AOQ. of ammunition, wagons drivers & teams/inf? Brigades under supervision of CRA. in Anti Tank demonstration near CAMBLAIN L'ABBE. 75 OR. reinforcements arrived in evening for DA and posted to Brigades	M-V.R M-V.R
	19 20 21 22 23.	12 noon	Road training programme conditioning of animals and lectures by CRA to officers of Divisional Artillery. ARP and Grenade dump taken over from 49th DAC. 30 G. wagons rejoined from 50L DAC. Operation orders received.	M-V.R M-V.R
	24	8 a.m.	51st DAC relieved 49th DAC in billets and lines at MADAGASCAR. E.A. active at 10am dropping propaganda Leaflets.	4-M.R
	25 26 27 28 29 30		Road fatigue with travelling to RE Infantry Brigades + DTMO. + taking mk. Enemy aircraft active especially on 27th & 29th. No damage done in DAC lines.	M-M

W.Shylton Major R.G.A (?)
Commdg 51st DAC

Vol 38

War Diary
October 1918
51st (Highland) Div. Amm. Col. RFA

Army Form C. 2118.

WAR DIARY
or
INTELLIGENCE SUMMARY.   51st D.A.C.
(Erase heading not required.)

Instructions regarding War Diaries and Intelligence Summaries are contained in F. S. Regs., Part II. and the Staff Manual respectively. Title pages will be prepared in manuscript.

Place	Date 1918	Hour	Summary of Events and Information	Remarks and references to Appendices
Tilloy	Oct. 1		51.D.A.C. at Bredagarn with Gun Dump in St Nicholas and S.A.A + Grenade Dump (Rcoeurg Dump) Normal fatigues.	Annex.
	2		Warning and Operation Orders received.	Annex.
	3		51.D.A.C. moves at 8.30 am via Haronsine to Agny - tec Suisans on being relieved by 8th D.A.C. Artiy Brigade dumps at Riecu Dump. A.R.P. and Grenade Dump handed over to 8th D.A.C.	Annex.
	4		Operation Orders received. 12 midnight.	Annex.
	5		At 5.45 am DAC moves via Arras and Arras-Cambrai Road to Cagnicourt, arriving at 10am	Annex.
	6		DAC left Cagnicourt at 5.30 pm arriving at Lichy-Ex-Artow at 6.30 pm. Very heavy amm. supply to Brigades, refilling at Thickon Dump, Bourlon. 3 O.R.s wounded, 1 horse killed a/c wounds.	Annex.
	7		Heavy ammunition supply. Improvement of lines etc.	Annex.
	8		Heavy ammunition supply.	Annex.
	9		Heavy ammunition supply.	Annex.
	10		Heavy ammunition supply.	Annex.
	11		51-DAC moves from Lichy and bivouacs via Bourlon-Raillencourt-Neuville-St-Remy on W of outskirts of Cambrai. No 2 Section delayed in route, owing to congestion of roads.	Annex.
	12		Wet morning. Heavy ammunition supply. Sump formed.	Annex.
	13		DAC moves at 8.30 am via Pont d'Aire to Escadoewres.	Annex.
	14		Heavy ammunition supply. Clearing ammunition from old battery positions. 50. Reinforcements to Sixth D.A.C.	Annex.
	15		Heavy ammunition supply. Clearing ammunition from old battery positions.	Annex.
	16		Do Do	Annex.

M Lewis White Lt Col.
Comdg 51 D.A.C.

Army Form C. 2118.

WAR DIARY
or
INTELLIGENCE-SUMMARY.
(Erase heading not required.)

51 D.A.C. (Continued)

Instructions regarding War Diaries and Intelligence Summaries are contained in F. S. Regs., Part II. and the Staff Manual respectively. Title pages will be prepared in manuscript. Sheet 2.

Place	Date 1918	Hour	Summary of Events and Information	Remarks and references to Appendices
Lieu	Oct. 17		Army Ammunition supply. Continued delivery of ammunition from old battery positions	Amiens.
	18		Do	Amiens.
	19		Ammunition supply normal. Interior Economy.	Amiens.
	20		Weather wet. D.A.C. moves from Escaudoeuvres to Lucy, leaving Escaudoeuvres 3.30pm arriving 5.30pm. New A.R.P. formed at N.11a (Sheet 51a)	Amiens.
	21		H.Q. No 1&2 Sections moved at 2.20pm from Lucy to Lieu R. Amand. New A.R.P. formed at I.27.C.	Amiens.
	22		5pm. S.A.A. Section moved from Lucy to Lieu R. Amand. Army ammunition supply. Weather Dull & Foggy.	Amiens.
	23		Delivering ammunition from old battery positions at Lucy and Avesnes-le-Sec.	Amiens.
	24		Army ammunition supply. New A.R.P. formed at I.7 Central.	Amiens.
	25		Weather normal. Employed clearing old positions and new dumps S.A.A. Section moved at 3.30pm to Souchy.	Amiens.
	26		H.Q. Nos 1 & 2 Sections moves from Neuville-Lyr-l'Escaut to Hauticken via Douchy, leaving at 11am and arriving at Hauticken. Enemy aircraft fairly active bombing Hud A.R.P. formed at I.22.C.26. No 1 Section shelled at Hauticken about 11pm. 5 animals wounded.	Amiens.
	27		H.Q. No 1 & 2 Sections moves from Hauticken to Neuville Sur l'Escaut and occupies new forward dumps. Army ammunition supply. Employed transporting ammunition from new to forward dumps.	Amiens.
	28		Weather normal. Forward dumps to be moved from present position to I.27.9b.2.5. North West of Hauticken on 29 October.	Amiens.
	29		Transporting from new to forward dumps. Delivering ammunition from vacated battery positions.	Amiens.
	30		Weather wet. Dump at I.27d. hourly shelled eg by A woods orders for personnel to return to J.7.c. (A.R.P.)	Amiens.
	31		SAA Section moves from Souchy to Lucy. Antique duty clearing up village streets in Neuville. Captain Rowlandson Lieut Holmes RGA Leaving 2/Lt (A/Capt) Rex Allen Lt RFA.

98.39

War Diary
51st D.A.C.
to
November 1918

WAR DIARY
or
INTELLIGENCE SUMMARY.
(Erase heading not required.)

Army Form C. 2118.

51st (H) DIVISIONAL
AMMUNITION COLUMN,
R.F.A.

Instructions regarding War Diaries and Intelligence Summaries are contained in F. S. Regs. Part II. and the Staff Manual respectively. Title pages will be prepared in manuscript.

Place	Date 1918	Hour	Summary of Events and Information	Remarks and references to Appendices
Field	Nov 1		HQ and Nos 1 and 2 Sections 50 DAC at Neuville sur L'Escaut (S.W. of Denain). S.A.A. Section at Iwuy (N.E. of Cambrai). 10 OR reinforcements arrived from First Army R.A Reinforcement Camp and posted to Bde.	Admin
	2		Improvement of billets &c.	Admin
	3		51st DAC (less S.A.A. Section) came under 56th D.A.	Admin
	W.5.6.		Issuing of ammunition. Heavy ammunition supply	9/18
	7		Detachment from 51st DAC took part in parade at Valenciennes on occasion of raise of Valenciennes publicly thanking First Army for the liberation of the town. HQ. Nos 1 and 2 moved at 15.45 round from Neuville to Saultrain (S.E. of Valenciennes).	1/18
	8	09.30	HQ 1 and 2 moved from Saultrain to Sebourquiaux via Estreux.	1/18
	9		HQ 1 and 2 moved across Belgian frontier to Angre	1/18
	10		HQ 1 and 2 moved from Angre to Audregnies. Heavy ammunition supply. S.A.A. Section moved to Neuville	1/18
	11.		HQ 1 and 2 moved from Audregnies & Sars La Bruyère. Hostilities ceased from 11.00 hours on signing of armistice with enemy	1/18
	12.		HQ 1 and 2 at Sars la Bruyère. S.A.A Section at Neuville	1/18
	13.	11.00	HQ 1 and 2 moves to Blaugies. 16 OR reinforcements arrived from First Army R.A Reinforcement Camp	1/18
	14.15		Improvement of billets &c. Local wagons engaged daily in transporting kit bags of repatriated french civilians from outlying villages to square in Blaugies where it was conveyed by lorries across frontier. This was continued daily till DAC left Blaugies. Soup kitchen also established in Blaugies for benefit of civilians.	H.Q.
	16	12.00	Personnel of HQ 1 and 2 with TM Personnel of HQ 51st DA addressed by G.O.C. 51st division in connection to Blaugies.	1/18.
	17:21		Improvement of billets, cleaning of equipment & preceded with in preparation for march into German territory.	1/18.
	22.		16 OR reinforcements posted to Brigade.	1/18.
	23.24.		Route fatigues; improvement of lines and billets.	1/18.
	25.	10.00	C.R.A. 51st division held inspection of DAC. This followed by march past and an exhibition of foot and sword drill.	Admin
	26.		Usual fatigues, cleaning of harness, wagons &c. Next to Germany postponed indefinitely.	Admin
	27	11.00	Operation order received. preparation completed for a move early the following morning	Admin
	28	06.30	HQ 1 and 2 moved from Blaugies, via Sars la Bruyère, Frameries and Mons to destination of Mignault, arriving at 16.00 hours.	Admin
	29.30		HQ 1 and 2 at Mignault. S.A.A. Section at Neuville. Improvement of billets started. commenced	Admin
			Weather during month showery, and roads in poor condition for heavy traffic.	

Anderson Lt.Col.
51.D.A.C.

War Diary
51st S.A.L.
to
December 1918

Army Form C. 2118.

WAR DIARY
or
INTELLIGENCE SUMMARY.
(Erase heading not required.)

Instructions regarding War Diaries and Intelligence Summaries are contained in F. S. Regs., Part II. and the Staff Manual respectively. Title pages will be prepared in manuscript.

51st (H) DIVISIONAL AMMUNITION COLUMN, R.F.A.
No. ....
Date ....

Place	Date 1918	Hour	Summary of Events and Information	Remarks and references to Appendices
FIELD.	Dec. 1.		HQ Nos 1 and 2 Sections in MIGNAULT (N.E. of MONS). Sqn Section at NEUVILLE SUR L'ESCAUT under 51st Division. Q. Improvement of billets stables, and carrying out of harness equipment rc.	1 T.S.K.
	2,3,4,5,6,7		Cleaning of harness, equipment rc. and grooming of animals, every animal being in covered stable.	1 T.S.K.
	8,9,10,11,12,13		Usual fatigue, cleaning of equipment rc.	1 T.S.K. / 1 T.S.C.
	14		Demobilization of coal miners, demobilizers & pivotal men commenced.	1 T.S.K.
	15,16		Usual fatigues.	1 T.S.K.
	17		9er reinforcement reports from First Army RA Reinforcement Camp, and attached to DAC pending disposal.	1 T.S.K.
	18		B or. reinforcements attached DAC pending disposal.	1 T.S.K.
	19		17 or. reinforcements posted to 78 Bde RFA. Usual daily fatigues	1 T.S.K.
	20		Usual fatigues & interior economy.	1 T.S.K.
	21,22,23,24,25		51st D.A.C. (less Sgn Section) moved from MIGNAULT to ECAUSSINES, MQ being established in ECAUSSINES'	1 T.S.K.
	26.	12.00	D'ENGHIEN & HQ/D2 Sections in ECAUSSINES CARRIÈRES. Improvement of stables rc. in new area. All route billets in private houses.	1 T.S.C.
	27		Usual fatigues cleaning of harness equipment rc.	
	28,29,30,31.		Weather during month wet, and roads in poor condition	1 T.S.C.

(signature) Lt. Col.
Commanding Highland Divisional. Ammn. Colmn.

98-41

51 DW

61

War Diary
of
51st JAB
for
January 1919

WAR DIARY
INTELLIGENCE SUMMARY

Army Form C. 2118.

Instructions regarding War Diaries and Intelligence Summaries are contained in F. S. Regs., Part II. and the Staff Manual respectively. Title pages will be prepared in manuscript.

(Erase heading not required.)

Place	Date 1919	Hour	Summary of Events and Information	Remarks and references to Appendices
Field	Jan. 1.		HQ., Nos. 1 & 2 Sections DAC in ÉCAUSSINNES. HQ situated in Grand'Place. SAA Section at NEUVILLE SUR L'ESCAUT under 51st Division "Q".	MSK
	2.		Naval fatigues.	MS & MSK
	3.		SAA section left NEUVILLE en route to rejoin DAC and arrived at ONNAING near VALENCIENNES in evening.	MSK
	4.		SAA section left ONNAING and marched to JEMAPPES (near MONS).	MSK
	5.		SAA completed fair trek and arrives at ÉCAUSSINNES at 15.00 hours. TM personnel and guns also arrives and taken on charge by DAC.	MSK
	6.7.8.9.		Stores of German ammunition equipment in area	MSK
	10.		CRA (II Corps) inspected lines, billets & of DAC in forenoon.	MSK
	11.		Continuation of salvage work in area, ammunition being taken to dump at ROEULX.	MSK
	12.13.14.15.			MSK
	16.		Naval fatigues.	MSK
	17.18.19.		Reclassification of animals for disposal.	MSK
	20.21.		Naval fatigues, cleaning of harness &c.	MSK
	22.23 &c.		28 animals evacuated to BOULOGNE for disposal.	MSK
	24.			MSK
	25.26.27.		Naval fatigues, sorting of ammunition &c, cleaning of harness equipment. Transport conditions difficult owing to hot and inconstant slippery condition of roads.	MSK
	28.29.30.			MSK
	31.		Weather during month dry but cold. Snow during latter part. Disposal of personnel proceeding, about 100 men being disposed during month.	MSK

H.B. Marshall Capt RAST.
OC H. Est Comm 5 S Div

Nd 4 B

Mary Doar
51st W.
Stat Bank
February 1919

Army Form C. 2118.

WAR DIARY
or
INTELLIGENCE SUMMARY.
(Erase heading not required.)

Sd/wr

Instructions regarding War Diaries and Intelligence Summaries are contained in F. S. Regs., Part II. and the Staff Manual respectively. Title pages will be prepared in manuscript.

Place	Date	Hour	Summary of Events and Information	Remarks and references to Appendices
FIELD	1919 FEB. 1		51st D.A.C. established at ECAUSSINNES. Ammunition (oblong) dump with charge of Dpt. of ROEULX Station. 2 Officers & 69 OR proceeded for disposal.	WS/K
	2,3,4,5		Transport difficult owing to bad frost & congested state of roads. Mud fatigues, care of animals, saddlery, equipment &c.	WS/K
	6,7		1 Officer 13 OR proceeded for disposal. Mud fatigue, saddling in area &c.	WS/K
	8			WS/K
	9,10,11, 12,13,14.		Care of animals, saddlery, equipment &c. Roads still bad & transport conditions difficult	WS/K
	15,16			WS/K
	17		Dump of ammunition &c. in area. 50 animals (C + C) - sold by auction at HOUDENG	WS/K
	18,19,20, 21		Mud fatigues & care of animals, saddlery &c.	WS/K
	22		1 Officer proceeded for disposal. Mud fatigues	WS/K
	23, 24, 25, 26		Mud fatigues & sorting of ammunition	WS/K
	27		11 OR proceeded for disposal.	WS/K
	28		Mud fatigues	WS/K
			Hard frost during first half of month renders transport conditions difficult. Snow fell not at frequent intervals.	WS/K

M—Roberts Lt Col
51st D.A.C.

Vol 43
51 Div

War Diary
51st Div
March 1919

Army Form C. 2118.

WAR DIARY
or
INTELLIGENCE SUMMARY.   51st D.A.C.
(Erase heading not required.)

Instructions regarding War Diaries and Intelligence Summaries are contained in F.S. Regs., Part II. and the Staff Manual respectively. Title pages will be prepared in manuscript.

Place	Date 1919	Hour	Summary of Events and Information	Remarks and references to Appendices
FIELD	Mar 1		51st D.A.C. in Billets at ECAUSSINNES in BELGIUM in process of reduction to cadre establishment. 106 animals (2) sent to MONS for entrainment to Base	M.A.K
	2,3,4		Road fatigues, working out of equipment &c.	1,2,3,K
	5		6 O.R. & 120 mules (X) & MONS for transfer to Army of Occupation in Germany	5/1/K
	6		Cleaning out of equipment &c.	1/6/K
	7		XVI Riders inspected by XXII Corps Horsemaster	4 & 5/7/K
	8		Road fatigues, cleaning up of equipment. Riders &c. 100 'x' mules to MONS for disposal	M.8.1.K
	9,10,11		Road fatigues, working out of equipment, clearing of harness &c.	1,9,10,K
	12,14			12,13,K
	15		D.A.C. wagons and stores & and to MANAGE during day to be placed in control of the base have been seen in by lorries — teams formed to D.A.C. by Brigades to take vehicles over. 3 O.R. to England for disposal	10,15,K
	16		Road fatigues	9,16,K
	17		50 2 animals to MONS for disposal	10,17,K
	18,19		Indented ammn. & Obs. spare transported to MONS. D.A.C. formed teams to Brigades — 255, 256, 260, (A) in turn — to be prepared & moved RH. vehicles to MANAGE and and to MONS.	M.18.K 19,1,K
	21,22		Indented ammn. of art at MANAGE. Transferred by lorry to MONS.	10,21,K 20,1,K
	23		Road fatigues &c	17,1,K
	24		5 riders (for re-purchase at home) sent to Base for transfer to England.	5,22
	25,26		Road fatigues, cleaning up, &c.	
	27		all remaining animals in D.A.C. (20 mules 23 L.D. & 24 mules) sent to MONS for disposal, all Indian personnel in D.A.C. (150 or) sent to MONS at night by lorry for entrainment to Indian Overseas Base Dept. ROUEN.	11,27,K
	28,29, 30,31		Road fatigues, &c, offices, riders at MANAGE Stas re.	11,31,K

Charles Robertson Lt.Col.
51st D.A.C.

www.ingramcontent.com/pod-product-compliance
Lightning Source LLC
Chambersburg PA
CBHW081429160426
43193CB00013B/2231